DOLLS & BEARS

TO MAKE AND DRESS

Australian Women's Weekly craft library

CONTENTS

MAKING DOLLS

Heirloom dolls, knitted dolls, rag dolls – there's something for everyone, sized from 36cm to 52cm

DOLLY DRESS-UPS

What every best-dressed doll and teddy will be wearing this year

MAKING BEARS

Knit a family of bears, or sew two very different teddies PLUS smart outfits to make

MAKING DOLLS

From exquisite heirloom dolls to
cute-as-a-button rag dolls, we show
you how to make dolls and clothes
to delight every child.

SWEET DREAMS

When dolls' heads and hands were first cast in porcelain, it made possible the lifelike appearance we presently take for granted and beautiful old porcelain dolls have become cherished antiques. Even today, they have the intrinsic value of all things fashioned by hand. Here, we show how to assemble your own heirloom doll, and dress her in finery to match.

MAKING A BABY DOLL

Instructions apply to making a doll with a purchased porcelain head and hands. We used a 52cm sleeping doll, "Sugar Britches", and her slightly smaller sister, "Gumdrop".

Measurements

Full-sized pattern pieces for Doll's Body and Doll's clothes, both graded in two sizes, are given on the pattern sheet, Side 3, in black.
Large _____
Small ....
Length (head to toe): 42cm (52cm)
Chest: 35cm (40cm)
Circumference of Head (measured around the forehead): 30cm (32cm)
Head height (chin to crown): 10cm (12cm)

Materials

■ One purchased porcelain head and hands, available from specialist doll shops. See page 120 for mail order suppliers
■ 0.4m fleecy-lined knit fabric for body parts. This is soft, easy to manipulate, and has the advantage of softening the feel of the pellets used for stuffing the doll's body
■ Cardboard
■ Craft glue
■ Plastic doll pellets – these approximate the weight of a baby of similar size, and thus add to the lifelike qualities of the doll

■ Polyfill padding, which is used in conjunction with the pellets and also helps to disguise their texture
■ Four shanked buttons, for extra support at hip and shoulder joints
■ Waxed dental floss, which makes marvellously strong, easy-to-use sewing thread for attaching limbs
■ 30cm x 0.90mm-gauge wire
■ Pliers
■ One extra-long sewing needle
■ Wig and eyelashes (optional)

Pattern pieces

All pattern pieces are printed on the pattern sheet, Side 3, in black. Trace Arm 9A, Leg 10A and Body 11A.

Cutting

Note. All pattern pieces *include* a 6mm seam allowance.

From fabric, cut four Legs, four Arms and two Body pieces.

Method

To prevent stuffing escaping into the head cavity, cut a disc of cardboard, sized to fit over the doll's neck opening, and glue in position.

With right sides facing, stitch Body pieces together, from centre back to centre front. Press under 12mm at neck opening, then narrowly turn in raw edge and stitch to form a casing with an opening at the back.

With right sides facing, stitch two Arm pieces together, leaving ends open. With Arm still wrong side out, place porcelain hand inside Arm, rim even with raw edge, fingers pointing towards shoulder end, and thumb pointing up.

Put a little glue on rim of hand and wind dental floss around fabric covering wrist to secure (*Diagram 1,* overleaf).

Turn Arm right side out through shoulder opening and fill with layers

of stuffing and pellets. Turn in seam allowance at shoulder and hand-stitch opening closed. Repeat for other Arm.

With right sides facing, sew two Leg sections together, leaving top open. Turn right side out and fill with layers of padding and pellets. Turn in seam allowance at hip and hand-stitch opening closed. Repeat for other Leg.

Stuff body with alternate layers of pellets and padding until it feels firm.

Thread wire through neck casing, put a little glue around the rim of the head and place it in the neck opening. Twist ends of wire at the back with pliers to secure and clip any excess. Hand-stitch opening closed.

Thread a long needle with four strands of dental floss, long enough to sew twice through the thicknesses of body and legs. Begin by sewing through one leg, leaving a length of thread trailing, through body at hip position, through second leg, through shank of button, back through leg and body and first leg, through shank of second button, to starting position (*Diagram 2*). Pull up strands tightly and tie ends together beneath button with a reef knot. Bury the ends of the floss in the leg. Position and stitch arms in the same way.

Glue on eyelashes and wig, if using. A couple of medium-sized elastic bands will be helpful to hold the wig firmly in position while the glue dries.

LEGGINGS

Materials

- 0.4m x 90cm lacy stretch knit fabric
- 0.7m x 3mm-wide ribbon

Pattern piece

Pattern piece is printed on the pattern sheet, Side 3, in black. Trace Front/Back 6A.

Cutting

Note. Pattern piece *includes* 1cm seam allowance.

From fabric, cut one Front/Back on fold.

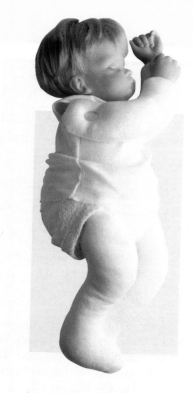

Diagram 1.

thumb on top

Diagram 2.

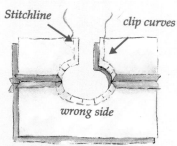

Diagram 3.

Stitchline *clip curves*

wrong side

two layers- yoke and yoke facing

Sewing

With right sides together, sew and neaten centre back seam. Pin fronts to backs at centre crotch and sew crotch, legs and foot seam through crotch, easing front feet where indicated. Turn in casing and sew. Thread ribbon through casing to tie around waist.

SHOES

Materials

- 0.2m x 90cm quilted fabric
- Bias binding to match
- Embroidery thread

Pattern pieces

Pattern pieces are printed on the pattern sheet, Side 3, in black. Trace Upper 7A and Sole 8A.

Cutting

Note. 1cm seam allowance is *included* on all pattern pieces.

From fabric, cut two Uppers and two Soles.

Sewing

With right sides together, pin and sew centre back seam.

Ease Upper edge with a row of long stitches, pull up to fit Sole, pin, tack and sew seam.

Sew bias binding around front curve of shoe.

Sew binding around back edge of shoe, leaving ties 21cm long on each side for tying.

Embroider rose buds on shoe front.

PETTICOAT

Measurements

To fit dolls 42cm tall, 35cm chest; (52cm tall, 40cm chest).

Materials

- 40cm batiste
- 1.10m lace edging
- One small press-stud

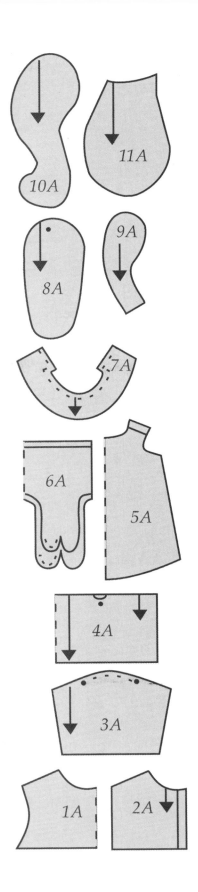

Pattern piece

Pattern piece is printed on the pattern sheet, Side 3, in black. Trace Front/Back 5A.

Cutting

Note. 1cm seam allowance is **included** on all pattern pieces.

From fabric, cut two Front/Backs.

Sewing

With right sides of Front and Back facing, sew French seams at sides and on one shoulder. (See Heirloom Dress with Yoke, below, for French seam method.) Turn under raw edges at neck and armholes and hand-stitch in position. Turn up 1cm at hem and sew on lace edging, trim fabric and neaten raw edge. Handsew ends of lace together to neaten. Sew hems on open shoulder and sew small press-stud on shoulder to close.

HEIRLOOM DRESS WITH YOKE

Measurements

To fit dolls 42cm tall, 35cm chest; (52cm tall, 40cm chest).

Materials

- 0.7m x 138cm Swiss voile
- 2.8m x 12mm-wide cotton lace insertion
- 3m x 22mm-wide cotton lace edging
- 1m x 13mm-wide ribbon
- 0.5m x 6mm-wide ribbon
- 4.2m entredeux (see **Note**)
- One reel fine machine embroidery thread
- Two 4mm buttons

Note. The "hemstitch" on either side of the lace insertion is achieved with a winged needle. If your sewing machine doesn't have such an attachment, you can achieve the same effect with entredeux lace, sewn between the lace insertion and fabric. While not an essential component of the dress, it is a traditional aspect of heirloom sewing and instructions for construction with entredeux lace are included.

Pattern pieces

All pattern pieces are printed on the pattern sheet, Side 3, in black. Trace Front Yoke/Front Yoke Facing 1A, Back Yoke/Back Yoke Facing 2A, Sleeve 3A and Skirt 4A.

Cutting

Note. 1cm seam allowance is **included** on all pattern pieces. From fabric, cut two Front Yoke/Front Yoke Facings, four Back Yoke/Back Yoke Facings, two Sleeves and one Skirt.

Sewing

With right sides together, sew Front Yokes to Back Yokes at shoulder seams. Repeat for Front and Back Yoke Facings. Place both yoke pieces with right sides together and sew up centre back, around neck and down opposite centre back seam (**Diagram 3**).

Trim, clip curves, turn right side out and press.

Leaving a 5cm opening for placket, make a French seam in centre back of skirt, that is, with wrong sides together, sew centre back seam of skirt, trim close to sewing and turn to bring right sides together.

Sew seam a second time, enclosing first seam.

If using machine hemstitch, sew a row of insertion lace at lower edge of skirt, about 1cm in from edge.

Sew three rows of pintucks, approximately 1cm above lace, and spaced approximately 1cm apart.

Sew second row of insertion lace above pintucks, then another three pintucks, as before.

Cut fabric from behind insertion lace, close to machine-stitching. With right side of fabric facing, overstitch lace borders with a close zigzag stitch or, for the hemstitched appearance of the original, use Machine embroidery thread and a winged needle to stitch: 44/2.5 (Janome), 165/2.0 (Pfaff), 26 Mirror Image (Bernina), D7 natural setting (Husqvarna), Hemstitching disc (Elna), or equivalent.

If using entredeux, sew a row of entredeux to lower edge of skirt, then insertion lace below entredeux.

Make three pintucks and cut around the skirt, approximately 6cm above top tuck. With right sides together, sew a row of entredeux to top edge of pin-tucked strip, join insertion lace to this entredeux and join another row of entredeux to the other side of insertion lace. With right sides together, join entredeux to top portion of skirt. Sew three more rows of pintucks above lace.

Slightly gather lace edging. Cotton lace has a thread that can be pulled for gathering.

With close zigzag stitch, sew the gathered lace edging to insertion lace on the lower edge of the skirt.

Turn under and hand-sew a small hem around back opening of skirt. Work two rows of gathering across top front and back between armholes.

Pull up gathers to fit yoke and, with right sides of yoke and skirt together, sew skirt to yoke.

Diagram 4.

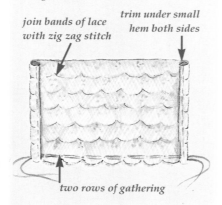

join bands of lace with zig zag stitch

trim under small hem both sides

two rows of gathering

Diagram 5.

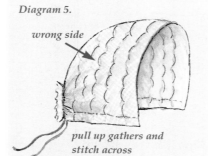

wrong side

pull up gathers and stitch across

Diagram 6.

Trim and neaten raw edge with oversewing.

Work two small buttonholes in right side of back and sew on buttons to correspond.

Sew on gathered lace edging at neck edge, turning in and handstitching ends to neaten.

On Sleeves, work two rows of gathering on armhole edge between dots. Make French seams in underarm seams. Draw up gathering to fit the armhole and sew in position (by hand, if it's too fiddly by machine). Trim and neaten.

On wrist edge of Sleeve, turn up 1cm to right side of fabric. Stitch lace edging over turn-up, 10mm from folded edge and again, as close to folded edge as possible. Thread the narrow ribbon through casing thus created and tie in bow. Hand-sew ends of lace together to neaten.

Sew on bow at centre front of yoke leaving the ends long.

BONNET

Measurements

To fit 30cm circumference head or 32cm circumference head.

Materials

■ 1.5m lace insertion
■ 60cm lace edging
■ 0.8m x 9mm-wide satin ribbon

Sewing

Cut lace insertion into five pieces, each 24cm long (or seven pieces, each 27cm long, for larger doll).

Sew lace edge-to-edge to create a rectangle. Roll a small hem on raw edges at sides of bonnet.

Run two rows of gathering stitches along one long side (**Diagram 4**). Pull up tight and secure gathering thread. With right sides together, fold in half and stitch across gathered end (**Diagram 5**). Turn to right side.

Butt the straight edges of the lace edging up against one another, with a slight overlap. Stitch the lace edging pieces together along the overlap and, using this row of stitching as a gathering thread, draw up edging to fit front edge of bonnet and stitch in place, forming a double-edged frill.

Stitch ribbon to bonnet along the junction of the lace edgings, folding and catching the ribbon in decorative pleats across the front, as shown (**Diagram 6**), and leaving ties at either end.

OH YOU BEAUTIFUL DOLL

Lizzie is absolutely everything a real rag doll should be – cute as a button, very soft and cuddly, and wearing lots of layers of pretty lace-trimmed clothes. She even has a little hankie in her pocket. Instructions for making Lizzie – and her clothes – start overleaf.

BEAUTIFUL RAG DOLL

Lizzie's gorgeous clothes, from underwear to a wonderful sunhat just right for summer, will fit any similarly sized doll.

Measurements

The finished doll is approximately 50cm (20") tall.

Materials

- 0.5m x 115cm calico
- 0.5m x 90cm white fabric, for underclothes
- 0.5m x 90cm fabric, for Dress
- 0.4m x 90cm fabric, for Pinafore
- 0.7m x 90cm fabric, for Hat
- 0.4m x 90cm iron-on interfacing
- 30cm square felt, for Shoes
- Polyester filling
- Two 1.5cm-diameter buttons
- Doll needle
- Strong thread
- 1.5m x 3cm-wide lace edging
- 0.8m x 4mm-wide elastic
- Small amount hat elastic
- Bias binding, for Collar piping (optional)
- 1.4m x 3cm-wide pre-gathered broderie anglaise
- Five Size 000 press-studs
- 0.6m x 1cm-wide lace edging, for Handkerchief
- Two 5mm-diameter pearl beads, for Shoes
- Pair of purchased Size 000 baby socks
- Two 13mm-diameter shank-style black buttons, for eyes
- Small amount dusty pink embroidery cotton
- Blusher or red pencil
- Dark brown pencil
- Wool for hair (we used 50g 12-ply mohair)
- Craft glue
- 1m x 1.5cm-wide ribbon, for hair ties

Pattern pieces

All pattern pieces, except rectangles, are printed on the pattern sheet, Side 2, in red. Trace Side Head 7, Centre Head 13, Front Body 12, Side Back Body 11, Centre Back Body 10, Arm 9, Leg 6, Foot 14, Knickers 8, Dress Front Bodice 16, Dress Back Bodice 15, Collar 5, Sleeve 4, Pinafore Front Bodice 3, Pinafore Back Bodice 17,

Pocket 18, Hat Crown 19, Hat Brim 20, Hat Side 2, Shoe Upper 1, Shoe Sole 21.

Cutting

Note. 6mm seam allowance and 1.5cm casing/hem allowance is *included* on all pattern pieces and given measurements, unless otherwise specified.

From calico, cut two Side Heads, one Centre Head, two Front Bodies, two Side Back Bodies, one Centre Back Body, four Arms, four Legs and two Feet.

From white fabric, cut two Knickers on the fold, one rectangle, 17.5cm x 90cm, for Petticoat, and one 12cm square for Hankie.

From Dress fabric, cut two Dress Front Bodices, two Dress Back Bodices on the fold, four Collars and two Sleeves on the fold. Cut also one rectangle, 18.5cm x 90cm, for Skirt.

From Pinafore fabric, cut two Pinafore Front Bodices on the fold, two Pinafore Back Bodices on the fold and two Pockets. Cut also one rectangle, 18.5cm x 80cm, for Skirt.

From Hat fabric, cut two Hat Crowns, two Hat Brims and one Hat Side.

From interfacing, cut one Hat Brim.

From felt, cut two Shoe Uppers and two Soles. Cut also two strips, each 8.5cm x 1cm, for shoe Straps.

Sewing

DOLL

Stitch dart in each Side Head and press dart to one side.

Stitch carefully just outside seam line of Centre Head and clip to stitching. With right sides together, pin Side Heads to Centre Head, matching notches, then stitch. Clip curves and turn right side out. Stuff head carefully and firmly, making sure that curves are evenly rounded. Set aside.

With right sides together, stitch centre front seam of Front Bodies.

With right sides together, stitch a Side Back Body to each side of Centre

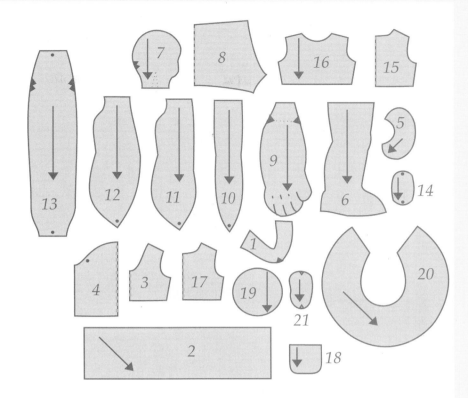

Back Body, matching small dots. With right sides together, stitch front to back at sides, leaving neck edge open. Clip curves and turn body right side out.

Stuff the body firmly and evenly. Run a strong gathering thread around raw neck edge and draw up gathers tightly, lacing across any exposed stuffing. Tie off thread securely.

Turn under raw edge on neck edge of head and baste to hold. Centre head over the gathered neck edge of body and, using double thread and small, neat stitches, stitch head firmly to body, inserting more stuffing into neck if necessary, before the seam is finally closed.

With right sides facing, stitch Arms together in pairs, leaving open above notches to make turning easier. Clip curves and turn right side out. Place a small amount of stuffing into lower end of Arm, then, either by hand or machine, stitch finger lines as shown on pattern. Tie off all threads securely and "bury" in Arm. Stuff Arm firmly as far as notches, turn in seam allowance on remaining raw edges and slipstitch neatly together.

Thread doll needle with strong double thread and knot ends. With

knot on underside of Arm, take a couple of stitches through small dot on upper Arm, emerging on outside of Arm. Thread needle up through one hole of button, across into second hole then through body of doll so that top edge of Arm sits about 1.5cm below neck seam. Squeeze body so that needle emerges at same position on opposite side of doll, then thread it through second Arm, through second button, and back across body to the starting position. Repeat this process a second time so that Arms are firmly secured, then tie off thread and "bury" ends in body.

With right sides together, stitch Legs together in pairs, leaving top and bottom edges open. Clip curves. Stay-stitch around lower edge of each Leg and clip to stitching. With right sides together, pin Feet to lower edges of Legs, matching dots to centre front and back seams. Baste and stitch. Clip curves and turn right side out.

Stuff Legs firmly and evenly. Turn in seam allowance on upper edges of Legs and slipstitch edges together, matching centre front and back seams. Position Legs on lower edge of body, along front/back seam line and stitch firmly in position with small, neat stitches, taking slight tucks in upper edge where necessary, so that each Leg fits between side edge and centre front seam.

It is easier to dress doll first, before adding face and hair.

UNDERCLOTHES

Knickers: Press under 6mm on leg edge of each Knicker piece. Cut a piece of 3cm-wide lace to fit each leg edge and, with edge of lace even with turned-in raw edge of Knickers, stitch lace to inside edge, about 3mm from fold. Cut a piece of hat elastic to fit along leg edge. Set machine to a wide zigzag-stitch. Lay elastic along inside edge of lace and zigzag in place, stitching carefully so that elastic is encased within zigzag but not caught. Leave elastic ends extending.

With right sides together, stitch inside leg seams, stitching across lace edging at the same time. Neaten seam with zigzag or overlocking. Pull up elastic to fit doll's legs and knot ends firmly to hold. Trim excess elastic.

With right sides together, stitch crotch seam from centre front to centre back, matching inside leg seams. Neaten seam.

Press under 5mm on upper raw edge, then turn under another 1cm and stitch to form casing, leaving an opening at centre back to thread elastic. Cut a piece of 4mm elastic to fit doll's waist, thread through casing, adjust to fit, secure ends, then stitch opening closed.

Petticoat: With right sides together, stitch short ends of Petticoat together to form centre back seam. Neaten edges and press seam open.

Press under 5mm on lower edge, then turn under another 1cm and stitch to form hem. Cut a piece of 3mm-wide lace to fit lower edge of Petticoat, plus turnings, and stitch in place on inside, as close as possible to lower edge. Neaten raw edges of lace by hand.

Press under 5mm on waist edge, then turn under another 1cm and stitch to form casing, leaving an opening at

centre back to thread elastic. Cut a piece of 4mm elastic to fit doll's waist, thread through casing, adjust to fit, secure ends, then stitch opening closed.

DRESS

If you are piping the Collar, cut two pieces of bias binding to fit around outside edge of Collar, allowing easing for curves, and press each in half lengthwise. With right sides together, baste binding to outer edge of Collar so that folded edge of binding will extend 2-3mm beyond seam when Collar is complete. With right sides together, stitch remaining Collar sections to piped sections, enclosing raw edges of binding. Clip curves, turn Collars right side out and press. (If you are not using piping, simply stitch the Collars together in pairs, turn right side out and press.)

With right sides facing, stitch Front and Back Bodices together at the shoulders to form one continuous piece. Press seams open and press Back Bodices in half along centre back fold lines so that one Front/Back Bodice section now forms bodice lining.

Baste Collars to Front Bodice, raw edges even and matching centre fronts. With right sides together, stitch bodice and bodice lining together at neck edge, sandwiching Collars at the same time. Clip curves, turn bodice lining back to inside and press. Baste the remaining raw edges of bodice and bodice lining together, matching the shoulder seams.

Run a gathering thread around upper edge of Sleeves. Test length of Sleeve on doll's arm and trim shorter if desired. (Pattern allows for a full-length sleeve. Our sleeve was not trimmed, but has a deep hem.)

Press under 4cm on lower edge of Sleeve and baste close to raw edge to hold. Cut broderie anglaise to fit lower edge and stitch to Sleeve, close to the folded edge. Cut a piece of 4mm elastic to fit doll's arm, plus seam allowance and, using zigzag and stretching elastic as you sew, stitch elastic to inside of Sleeve, covering raw edge of Sleeve hem at the same time. Remove basting.

With right sides together, pin Sleeve to armhole edge, draw up gathers to fit and stitch. Neaten seam. Repeat for remaining Sleeve.

With right sides together, stitch side and Sleeve seams in one continuous operation, stitching across broderie anglaise and securing ends of elastic at the same time. Neaten seam.

With right sides facing, stitch short ends of Skirt together to form centre back seam, leaving 6cm open at waist edge. Press the seam open, including edges of opening.

Press under 5mm on lower edge of Skirt, turn under another 1cm to form hem, stitch. Cut a piece of broderie anglaise to fit lower edge of Skirt, plus turnings, and stitch in position, turning under raw ends at centre back and neatening by hand.

Run two rows of gathering threads around waist edge and draw up gathers to fit bodice.

With right sides together, pin Skirt to

bodice and stitch, allowing a 1cm seam. Trim and neaten the seam.

Sew three small press-studs to centre back to close.

PINAFORE

With right sides facing, stitch Front and Back Bodices together at shoulders to form one continuous piece. Press seams open and press Back Bodices in half along centre back fold lines so that one Front/Back Bodice section now forms bodice lining.

With right sides together, stitch bodice and bodice lining together around neck and armhole edges, leaving side seams open.

Clip curves, turn right side out and press. Open out sides so that underarm seams and waist edges match on each side and sew side in one long seam.

Press under 5mm on each short edge of Skirt, then turn under another 1cm

and stitch. Make a similar hem on one long edge of Skirt. Run two gathering threads along remaining raw edge of Skirt and draw up gathers to fit bodice. With right sides together, pin bodice to Skirt, keeping bodice lining free, adjust gathers and stitch, allowing a 1cm seam. Turn under raw edge of bodice lining and slip-stitch in place over seam.

Press 1.5cm facing allowance to outside on upper edge of each Pocket and stitch at sides, continuing stitching around Pocket on seam line. Turn facing back to inside, clip across seam allowance to stitching and press seam allowance under on stitching line. Position Pockets on front of Pinafore and top-stitch in place.

Using a close, narrow zigzag-stitch, sew 1cm-wide lace to edges of 12cm white square, folding mitres into corners as you go. Neaten mitres and raw edges of lace by hand. Fold Hankie and place in pocket.

Sew two small press-studs to centre back edge of bodice.

HAT

With right sides together, stitch short ends of Hat Side and press seam open. Press Side in half lengthwise, wrong sides together, matching seams, and baste raw edges to hold. Run a line of ease-stitching around raw edges of Hat Side.

With wrong sides facing, baste Hat Crowns together.

With right sides facing, baste and stitch Crown to raw edges (not folded edge) of Hat Side, pulling up ease-stitching to accommodate fullness, and distributing fullness evenly so that there are no tucks in seam line. Neaten seam.

Apply interfacing to wrong side of one Brim piece. With right sides together, join short ends of Brim and press seam open. Repeat for remaining

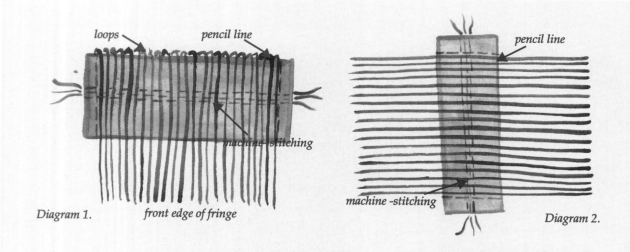

loops · pencil line

machine-stitching

Diagram 1.

front edge of fringe

pencil line

machine-stitching

Diagram 2.

Brim piece which becomes Brim Lining.

With right sides together, stitch Brim to Brim Lining around outer edge. Turn right side out and press. Stitch raw edges of Brim and Lining together, following seam line. Clip across seam allowance to stitching around inner edge of Brim. Position folded edge of Hat Side over inner edge of Brim, using stitching line as a guide, and baste. Top-stitch close to folded edge of side.

Neaten seam and press towards Side, then top-stitch again, about 5mm apart.

SHOES

With right sides together, stitch centre back seam of Shoe, stitching 2-3mm from edge.

With right sides together, stitch Sole into Shoe – you might find it easier to do this by hand, as it's rather fiddly. Round one end of each Strap, fold the tip back on itself and cut a tiny nick with scissors, to form buttonhole. Stitch remaining end of Strap to inside of Shoe, positioning it slightly diagonally so that it will sit snugly across doll's instep. Sew a small pearl to each outer side, so that the Strap can be buttoned.

FACE

Using a doll needle and strong thread, and anchoring thread at back of head, stitch black buttons to face for eyes, pulling them slightly to create

eye sockets. Tie off threads securely. Ends will be hidden by hair.

Using two strands of dusty pink embroidery cotton, work a simple curved mouth in stem-stitch. Using one strand of dusty pink, work a smaller curve in backstitch as a nose.

Rub a little blusher or red pencil onto cheek areas and dot lightly across nose and below eyes with a sharp brown pencil for freckles.

HAIR

Cut a piece of calico on the bias, about 13cm x 6cm. Lay this strip across the top of doll's head at fringe level, and mark head seam lines with a pencil.

Cut a number of 25cm lengths of wool and fold in half. The exact number will depend on how thick you want the fringe to be, but you need enough to fit side by side along the length of your bias strip, between the pencil lines.

Using a little craft glue, position the folded wool lengths across bias strip, having loops even with one long edge, and the other ends extending beyond the opposite edge.

Using a matching machine thread, stitch along the centre of the bias strip, to secure wool, then stitch again, a couple more times, close to the first line of stitching – this will ensure that wool is securely held (see *Diagram 1*). Set aside.

Now cut another bias strip, about

6cm x 20cm, and mark pencil lines across each end of strip, about 2cm from the end. Cut the remainder of your wool into 70cm lengths and arrange across strip, between pencil lines, this time so that strip lies in centre of wool and wool ends extend evenly on each side. Glue and stitch as before (*Diagram 2*).

Fold under and glue front raw edge of fringe strip almost back to the stitching line. Spread craft glue thoroughly over underside of strip and glue in position across top of head, so that folded edge sits approximately where you imagine the hairline would be, and matching pencil lines to seams. The fringe will probably be too long at this stage, but can be trimmed later. Allow this to dry.

Fold under extending raw ends at each end of longer strip, so they are completely concealed, and glue in place. Position this strip down the centre back of the doll's head, so that the top edge is even with the fringe stitching line and completely covers the looped ends, and the lower edge sits about 4cm above the nape of the neck. Glue firmly in place.

Lift hair out of the way and lightly pencil a hairline around sides and lower back of head. Spread glue fairly liberally over head, following hairline and press hair firmly into glue.

When dry, trim fringe (not too evenly) and arrange hair into plaits, trimming ends even and tying with matching hair ribbons.

GOLLY GOSH

If you're 30-something or a little older, it's likely you'll have your own fond memories of a childhood golly – knitted or stitched, with his bright clothes and cheerful grin, he was always a colourful counterpart to ted's gruff demeanour. Now a new generation can enjoy Golly. Instructions start overleaf.

MAKING A GOLLY

Measurements

Finished golly is approximately 40cm tall.

Materials

8-ply wool (50g):
- Two balls black
- One ball each red, yellow, blue
- Small amount of green, for Bow-tie
- One pair 3mm (No 11) knitting needles
- Tapestry needle
- Polyester filling
- Two red and two yellow - buttons (2.5cm diameter), for Trousers
- Medium-sized crochet hook
- Four gold buttons
- Small amount 6mm-wide black elastic
- black press-stud
- Scraps of black, red and white felt

Abbreviations: See Knitting and Crochet Notes on page 120.

Body/Head (make 2)

Note. Work in st st throughout.

Using black yarn and 3mm needles, cast on 32 sts.

Work 13cm st st, ending with a purl row.

Cast off 8 sts at beg of next 2 rows...16 sts.

Work 4 rows for neck.

Increase one st at each end of every row until there are 38 sts.

Cont until Head measures 6.5cm from top of neck, ending with a purl row. Dec one st at each end of every row until 10 sts rem.

Cast off.

Legs (make 2)

Using black yarn and 3mm needles, cast on 35 sts. Work 4cm garter st.

Next row. K11, cast off next 13 sts, knit to end...22 sts.

Next row. P22.

Cont in st st for rem, inc one st at each end of 5th and every foll 4th row until there are 30 sts.

Cont until Leg measures 15cm in all. Cast off.

Arms (make 2)

Using black yarn and 3mm needles, cast on 22 sts. Work 11.5cm st st, ending with a purl row.

Next row. (K2 tog) to end of row. Break off yarn, thread end through rem sts, draw up and fasten off.

Hair

Using black yarn and 3mm needles, cast on 49 sts. Knit 2 rows. Beg patt.

1st row. *K1, insert needle into next st, pass yarn twice round needle and first two fingers of left hand in clockwise direction, then round needle once, draw all 3 loops through, replace them on lefthand needle and knit them all tog through the back of the sts; rep from * to last st, K1.

2nd row. Knit.

These 2 rows form patt. Cont until work measures 5cm, ending with a 2nd row.

Cast off 18 sts at beg of next 2 rows...13 sts.

Cont in patt, dec one st at each end of 3rd and every foll 4th row until all sts are worked off.

Jacket
(worked in one piece)

Beg at waist edge of Back. Using blue yarn and 3mm needles, cast on 28 sts. Work 2.5cm garter st, ending with a wrong side row.

Cast on 8 sts for underarm seam at beg of next 6 rows...76 sts. Cont until work measures 7cm in all, ending with a wrong side row.

Next row. K29, cast off next 18 sts for back of neck, knit to end.

Next row. K29, cast on 16 sts for front neck. Cont on these 45 sts until sleeve measures 10cm, ending with a right side row.

Cast off 8 sts at beg of next and foll 2 alt rows (side edge)...21 sts.

Cont until side edge measures 2.5cm from underarm. Dec one st at each end of every row until 3 sts rem. K3tog and fasten off. With wrong side facing, rejoin yarn to rem 29 sts, cast on 16 sts, complete to correspond with first side.

Trousers (make 2)

Beg at inner leg seam. Using red yarn and 3mm needles, cast on 26 sts. Knit 1 row (wrong side).

Cont in garter st, in stripes of 2 rows yellow, 2 rows red, work 6 rows, inc one st at beg of 1st, 3rd and 5th rows...29 sts.

Cast on 17 sts at beg of next row. Cont until work measures 13cm from where the 17 sts were cast on, finishing after 2 rows yellow.

Cast off 17 sts at beg of next row, work to end.

Work 6 rows, dec one st at beg of 2nd, 4th and 6th rows...26 sts.

Knit 1 row with red.

Cast off.

Braces (make 2)

Using red yarn and 3mm needles, cast on 7 sts.

Work in garter st for 23cm.

Cast off.

Bow-tie

Using green yarn and 3mm needles, cast on 8 sts.

Work in garter st for 20cm.

Cast off.

TO MAKE UP

With right sides facing, stitch Head/Body sections together, leaving lower edge open, and fill head and

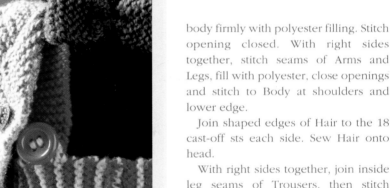

body firmly with polyester filling. Stitch opening closed. With right sides together, stitch seams of Arms and Legs, fill with polyester, close openings and stitch to Body at shoulders and lower edge.

Join shaped edges of Hair to the 18 cast-off sts each side. Sew Hair onto head.

With right sides together, join inside leg seams of Trousers, then stitch crotch seam. Using yellow yarn and crochet hook, make two 10ch lengths for button loops, leaving a length of thread at each end. Stitch these ends to front of Trousers, approximately 3cm either side of centre front.

Attach Braces to inside back edge of Trousers, with two large yellow buttons. Place Trousers on Golly, cross Braces and bring to front over shoulders, then sew two red buttons to Braces to match button loops.

With right sides together, join seams of Jacket, stitch upper corners down to form collar, and trim front with four gold buttons.

Join ends of Bow-tie together to form a circle, place seam at centre back, then bind green yarn around centre of loop to create a bow-tie effect. Secure ends.

Attach a black press-stud to each end of a piece of elastic to fit Golly's neck, then attach one end of elastic to back of Bow-tie. Clip around Golly's neck. Cut facial features from felt scraps, following the photograph, and stitch or glue in place.

This charming traditional golly is knitted quickly in simple stocking stitch and, with his removable garter stitch clothes, is sure to be a special favourite with today's children.

THREE LITTLE MAIDS

Each member of this charming trio, with their sweet expressions and old-fashioned clothes, has an appeal that will captivate all ages – especially those between eight and eighty. They're all made and dressed from the same basic pattern but, as you can see, the possibilities for variety are endless.

Collette

BASIC RAG DOLL BODY

Measurements

Each doll is 36cm tall.

Materials

▪ 30cm flesh-coloured cotton fabric (see **Note**)
▪ Polyester fibrefill
▪ Strong pink quilting thread, for assembling bodies
▪ Fabric paints or stranded embroidery thread, in dark brown, white, black, light brown, dark flesh and coral pink
▪ Toothpick or small paintbrush
▪ Red and brown coloured pencils
▪ Fine point brown permanent marker, for freckles
▪ Clear-drying craft glue (optional)
Note. The best fabric for bodies is tightly woven cotton, such as unbleached calico or homespun. It can be dyed a flesh colour with a *tiny* amount of Dylon Tangerine dye. Do not use a cotton polyester blend, as the fabric will not "give" and wrinkles will form at curves and stress points.

Pattern pieces

All the pattern pieces, except the rectangles, are printed in a panel on the pattern sheet, Side 4, in black.

Trace Head Back, Head Front, Side Head, Ear, Body Front, Body Back, Leg, Arm and Foot Sole.

Cutting

Note. All pattern pieces *include* 3mm seam allowance.

From flesh-coloured fabric, cut one Head Back, one Head Front, two side Heads, four Ears (Kathleen only), one Body Front, two Body Backs, four Legs, four Arms amd two Foot Soles.

Sewing

When joining pieces, place right sides together, unless otherwise directed.

Join Head Back to Head Front along top edge. Join this central head piece to Head Sides, making sure to sew smoothly around curves. Leave open at neck edge.

Turn right side out through neck opening, taking care as opening is small.

Sew Body Back pieces together along centre back, leaving open, as indicated on pattern. Sew Body Front to Body Back, leaving open only at neck. Turn right side out.

Sew Arms together in pairs, leaving top edge open. Turn right side out.

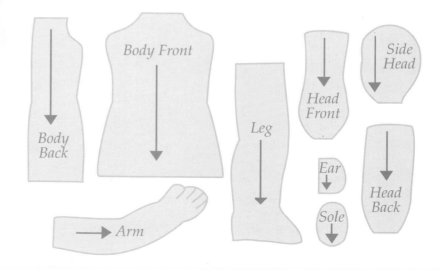

Sew Legs together in pairs along the centre front and back seams, leaving open at top and bottom. Make tiny clips along sole edge of feet, then pin and tack Foot Soles in position. Sew, then turn right side out.

Sew the Ears together in pairs around the curved edges, leaving straight edges open. Turn right side out.

Fill head very firmly with polyester fibrefill. To achieve a smooth, firmly packed effect, use a stuffing stick, such as a paintbrush handle, rounded pencil or chopstick. Do not use any implement with a pointed end. Check frequently from all angles that the head is symmetrical and not pushed out of shape. Push small amounts of filling into chin area for a rounded, rather than square appearance.

There should be no wrinkles and the head should be firm enough to withstand handling without any dents appearing.

Fill body firmly and smoothly. Use the stuffing stick to ensure that the neck is completely filled out. When body is filled, sew closed the opening in the centre back.

Fill hands softly and topstitch fingers, as indicated on pattern, by hand or machine. Fill arms firmly up to 2cm from top, leaving remainder empty. Turn in raw edges and sew closed.

Sculpt inside of wrist, if desired, with one long stitch, pulled tightly from seam to seam.

Fill legs firmly up to top. If you want the doll to sit easily, leave the top 2cm of legs empty. Turn in raw edges, matching centre front seam to centre back seam, and sew legs closed.

Place head over neck, facing centre front. Brace the body against your chest and press down firmly on head to hold in place. Sew twice around with quilting thread, making tiny stitches and pulling stitches tight. Tuck in raw edges with the point of needle as you sew. Neck should be shorter at front than back. Place arms at shoulders and sew in position. Legs are

Diagram 1.

Diagram 2.

sewn to bottom seam of the body.

Before applying the doll's face, you might like to read the tips for Making a Doll's Face, on page 26.

Facial features may be sketched freehand, using a brown coloured pencil. Sketch lightly until you are happy with the placement of the features.

Mistakes can be removed with a white eraser.

Alternatively, trace the features from **Diagram 1** (Kathleen) or **Diagram 2** (Collette or Holly) onto a small piece of paper, using a sharp transfer pencil.

Position the paper carefully on the face, noting that eyes will be halfway down the face.

Pin paper securely to face and check that eyes are level and mouth is on vertical centre line of face. Iron onto face, then proceed to paint or embroider features as follows.

A combination of fabric paint and embroidery thread is used for the features. Permanent markers (with fine tip) are also ideal substitutes for paint. If you are using fabric paint, a toothpick gives excellent control for fine lines – much easier than a brush. Our dolls' eyes are either blue or brown, with black pupils. The outline of the eye, eyelid and lashes are also brown. The eyebrows are brown lines (either marker or embroidery).

Two rows of dark flesh stemstitch are used for the nose, while the lips are filled in with satin-stitch in coral pink. Use one strand of embroidery thread.

Dot freckles across nose area with a sharp brown pencil, permanent marker or a pin dipped in fabric paint.

To make rosy cheeks, scribble on a scrap of paper with red pencil, then rub the paper in a circular motion on the cheek area.

To make white highlights in eyes, thread a long needle with white thread (two strands), anchor the thread at side of head behind hairline, then push needle through head into eye, make a tiny straight stitch, then return to starting place.

Pull slightly on thread to create eye socket (not so hard that wrinkles appear), then fasten off thread. Repeat for other eye.

Fill ears (for Kathleen) softly with fibrefill, turn in raw edges on straight sides, and stitch closed by hand. Topstitch by hand or machine, 3mm inside curved edge of ear.

Position ear on side of head, noting that the top of the ear should be level with eyebrow and straight edge of ear is about 2cm back from side seam.

Stitch ear to head from top to bottom. Tack ear to head with a couple of stitches concealed behind ear, or craft glue.

THE CLOTHES

Materials

■ One basic doll, with ears
■ 0.4m white cotton fabric (such as lawn or batiste) for underwear
■ 0.2m light cotton print fabric for blouse
■ 0.3m dark cotton print fabric for pinafore
■ Scrap of fine voile for collar
■ 20cm, or remnant, cream knit fabric for stockings
■ Scraps of beige and cream felt for shoes
■ 2.25m x 2cm cotton lace edging
■ 0.5m x 3mm elastic
■ 5-ply apricot yarn for hair (see **Note**)
■ 0.6m x 2cm satin ribbon for hair
■ Six small press-studs
■ 0.75m x 3mm silk ribbon for collar
■ Small amount narrow ribbon for shoes
■ Crochet cotton for shoe ties
■ Two tiny pearl beads for ear studs
Note. If 5-ply yarn is hard to find, crewel wool is an excellent substitute. You will need five or six skeins for a long hairstyle.

Pattern pieces

All pattern pieces, except rectangles, are printed in a panel on the pattern sheet, Side 4, in black. Trace Petticoat Bodice Front/Back, Pants Front/Back, Blouse Front/Back, Blouse Sleeve, Pinafore Bodice Front/Back, Stocking, Shoe Upper, Shoe Sole and Collar A.

Cutting

Note. All pattern pieces **include** 3mm seam allowance.

From white cotton fabric, cut two Pants Front/Backs, two Petticoat Fronts on fold, four Petticoat Backs and one 15cm x 50cm rectangle for petticoat skirt.

From light cotton print, cut one Blouse Front on fold, two Blouse Backs and two Blouse Sleeves.

From dark cotton print, cut two Pinafore Bodice Fronts on fold, four Pinafore Bodice Backs and one 15cm x

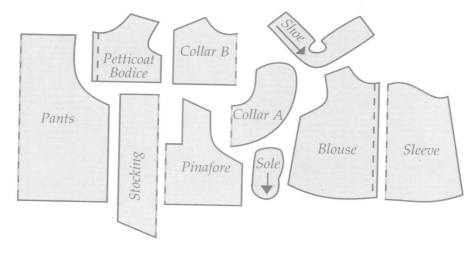

70cm rectangle for pinafore skirt.

From voile, cut two Collars A.

From cream knit fabric, cut two Stockings.

From cream felt, cut two Shoe Uppers.

From beige felt, cut two Shoe Soles.

Sewing

KATHLEEN

Hair

On basic doll with ears, mark hairline lightly on the head with brown pencil (see **Diagram 3**).

Cut 45cm strands of apricot wool. Thread a large-eyed needle with one strand of yarn and pull it through on the hairline (see **Diagram 3**). Knot the strands together tightly on the hairline. Continue this procedure until the entire hairline is covered.

Pull all strands to top of head and tie tightly with yarn. Trim ends of pony-tail, if desired. Knot a few short strands to the hairline at the forehead and trim as desired, for a fringe. Tie the 2cm-wide ribbon in a bow on the ponytail.

Clothes

When joining pieces, place right sides together, unless otherwise directed.

Pants: Machine-stitch a narrow hem on the leg and waist edges of Pants. Stitch the centre front seam. Sew flat lace edging to the leg edges.

Using a long zigzag stitch, sew flat 3mm elastic to legs and waist, close to hem, stretching elastic as you sew. Stitch centre back and inner leg seams.

Petticoat: Stitch the Petticoat Front to Petticoat Backs at the shoulders (one set will form petticoat lining).

With right sides facing, stitch centre back edges, neck edge and armholes, leaving side seams open. Clip curves, taking care not to cut stitching, then turn right side out and press. Open out sides so that underarm seams and waist edges match on each side and sew through in one long seam.

Turn under the raw edge on one long edge of the skirt rectangle and stitch. Attach flat lace to this edge, just under the stitched edge – two rows of lace may be used, if desired.

Sew short edges of skirt together, leaving top half open. Machine a narrow hem on open edges, for placket. Run a gathering thread around waist edge of skirt. Pull up gathers to fit bodice and stitch, folding lining out of the way.

Hem the lining over the raw edges on the inside of the skirt. Attach two small press-studs at the back opening: one at the neck and one at the waist.

Blouse: Turn under raw edges on the cuff end of Sleeves and stitch. Attach flat lace. Stitch the Front to Backs at shoulder seams.

Gather tops of Sleeves slightly to fit armholes and stitch Sleeves in place. Attach elastic to Sleeves just above lace, as for Pants. Sew underarm and side seams. Machine-stitch a narrow

HANDMADE
Magazine

Contemporary craft, classic
and country decorating,
elegant gifts and other
beautiful things to make.

WILTSHIRE SCISSORS
with every gift
subscription!

*only $4.75 per copy
by subscribing*

Handmade is more than a
collection of the prettiest projects
and clever short-cuts,
it's also a storehouse
of great craft and decorating ideas.

When you subscribe,
all this is delivered
right to your door
SIX times a year –
and the delivery is
absolutely **FREE**.
Don't miss a
single issue – subscribe today!

Have you discovered Australia's best craft magazine, **Handmade**? **Handmade** is The Australian Women's Weekly's own bi-monthly craft magazine and, as its name implies, is completely devoted to patterns and projects that you can make yourself. We cover the whole range of handiwork from fashion sewing and sewing for the whole family (**with free patterns in every issue**), through to the most exciting and beautiful handknit patterns and every sort of needlework and craft you might care to make.

Here's just a sample of what we offer:

- Delightful needlework projects – cross-stitch, tapestry, crewel, ribbon, wool and hardanger work, for example – with a range to suit from beginners to more adventurous needleworkers, looking for a challenge.
- Environmentally and economically sensible crafts where something new is crafted "from nothing", or at least without busting the budget – such as wardrobe makeovers, rag rugs, paper and basket-making.
- Quick craft and gift ideas – for fetes and seasons of giving.
- Beautiful painted finishes and folk art to brighten your home.
- Cottage and country crafts and traditional crafts revisited.
- No-one offers a more comprehensive range of soft toys to make – traditional, modern, country, fantasy – all with child appeal.
- New craft products introduced and put to use in lots of terrific projects for home and family.
- Homemaking skills – time-honoured "recipes" for making slipcovers, curtains, cushions and other soft furnishings.
- Special crochet projects – whether it's as large as a bedcover or as elegant as a pretty collar.

Because we are a magazine devoted solely to hand-crafted projects, we have space in our packed 112 pages to cover things **comprehensively**, often with step-by-step illustrations. If you would like to see more of what **Handmade** has to offer, then subscribe **now**. For only $4.75 per issue (rrp is $5.95!), Australia's best craft magazine can be delivered to your door, POST FREE, six times a year – with our special subscriber's gift to you, a handy pair of Wiltshire scissors.

No postage stamp required if posted in Australia

The Australian Women's Weekly
HANDMADE
CRAFT · DECORATING · FASHION

REPLY PAID 764
HANDMADE
GPO Box 5252
SYDNEY NSW 1028

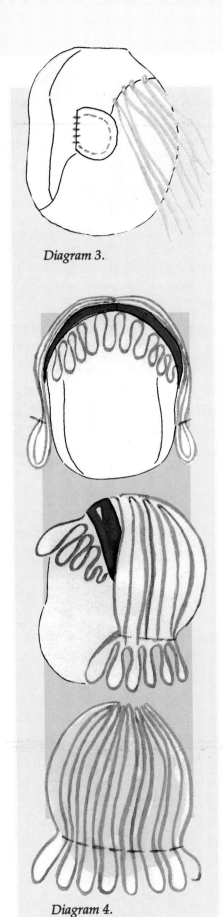

Diagram 3.

Diagram 4.
Holly's hairstyle.

hem on the lower edge of the blouse.

Cut a narrow bias strip of the blouse fabric and bind the neckline of the blouse. Stitch a press-stud at the neck edge of the back opening.

Pinafore dress: Construct the Pinafore Bodice and Skirt in the same manner as the Petticoat, omitting the reference to lace. Try the Pinafore on the doll and pin the skirt up so that the lace on the petticoat shows beneath the dress skirt. Hem skirt by hand.

Close centre back at neck and waist.

With right sides together, stitch Collars together, leaving about 3cm unsewn on outer curved edge for turning. Turn right side out and press. Turn in raw edges of opening and stitch closed. Slightly gather lace edging to fit the outer curved edge of collar, then neatly sew lace to the collar, by machine or hand, with edge of the lace just under the outer edge.

Handsew the silk ribbon in place near the collar edge. Tie a bow with long ends and stitch to the centre front of the collar. Close the collar at the back with a press-stud.

Stockings: Fold Stockings in half lengthwise and stitch seams from toe to heel and up back of leg. Turn right side out and pull onto the doll's leg – the leg will mould stocking to shape.

Shoes: Sew the centre back seam of the Shoe Uppers by hand, using a small blanket stitch. Gather the toe area of the Upper to fit the Sole, then sew the Soles to Uppers, with the centre back seam of the Upper matching the heel. Turn right side out.

Stitch a tiny ribbon bow to the front of each shoe, and thread a piece of crochet cotton through Upper to tie the shoe at the ankle.

Stitch pearls to earlobes, for earrings.

COLLETTE

Collette is made and dressed in the same way as Kathleen with the following variations:

Make the basic body, but cut the Legs from 25cm striped cotton fabric – stockings will not be needed.

Her face is similar to Kathleen's, but her eyes are blue and she does not have ears.

To make her hair, you will need 5-ply sandy-coloured yarn. Draw the front hairline across her head, about 2.5cm above eyebrows. Sew a row of yarn loops across the forehead. Cut strands of yarn, 42cm long. Drape across the head, so that the ends hang down evenly on each side.

Using matching thread, stitch hair securely to the head in the centre parting, from the forehead to the nape of the neck. Stop about 2cm above the neck seam.

Cut a few extra 42cm strands, fold each in half and sew the looped ends to the front hairline. These strands are pulled straight back.

Gather the yarn into two bundles at ear level. Tie with yarn and stitch securely to the head. Plait the yarn tightly and tie the ends of the plaits. Trim to the desired length and tie a bow on each plait at ear level.

Leave sufficient ribbon to make a small matching bow for the collar. You will need 1m x 10mm ribbon, instead of the silk ribbon for Kathleen.

Collette's underwear is made of cream lawn, trimmed with cream lace.

Her clothing is identical to Kathleen's except that Collar B is used and is made of same fabric as blouse.

Her pinafore is trimmed with a strip of blouse fabric, 70cm x 2.5cm.

Her Shoes are made as for Kathleen, except that 3mm ribbon is used for ties, and bow on shoe front is omitted.

HOLLY

Holly has the same face as Kathleen, and is made with the following variations:

Her underwear is white lawn, with broderie anglaise trim. Stockings are made from red ribbed stretch fabric (use an old pair of tights). Her Collar is Collar A, trimmed with broderie anglaise. Her Blouse is dark green and her pinafore is tartan, trimmed with a ribbon at the waist.

For the sash and hair band, you will

need 1m x 12mm satin ribbon. Her Shoes are black felt, tied with 3mm black ribbon.

To make her hair, you will need dark brown fluffy yarn, such as a mohair blend. With matching thread, sew loops of yarn across the front hairline (see **Diagram 4**).

Loop yarn across the top of the head and down the sides. Do not cut the ends. Keep the loops even at the bottom. Stitch the yarn to the head at the sides, 2cm up from the looped ends. Pull the thread tight so that it sinks into the fluffy yarn and is not visible.

Sew a centre part at the top of the head. When the top of the head is covered, tie a ribbon band around head and knot at back of head (hair will cover knot at back).

Continue to loop yarn from crown of head to neck and sew loops down, as before.

MAKING A DOLL'S FACE

No amount of careful sewing or exquisite costuming will make up for a doll whose face is ugly or unappealing, so it's worth taking the time and trouble to get it right.

Facial features can be painted or embroidered. To determine appropriate shape of eyes, nose and mouth, draw a few of each on scraps of fabric, cut out and pin to doll's face. Move and change the expression until you are satisfied.

Having decided on design and placement of features, transfer them to the face by tracing design onto thin paper with a transfer pencil and then ironing onto the face in the correct position. You can also draw features freehand with a coloured pencil or water-erasable pen.

Embroidery is easier to do after head is filled, as cloth will be stretched taut. Use one strand of thread for fine lines or very small dolls. Use two

or three strands for filling in areas or for larger dolls.

If you are using ball-point fabric paints, paint face before making up the head, as these paints need to be pressed onto a firm surface.

For permanent fabric paints that do not have this requirement, a toothpick makes a good applicator.

Ordinary coloured pencils can be used for drawing features – just moisten pencil to make colours more intense. A sparing coat of nail varnish will seal colours and prevent them washing out.

Whichever method you choose, practise first on a scrap of body fabric to check if the colours run.

Most dolls look better with rosy cheeks. The best blusher is a red, pink or orange coloured pencil, as this does not run, bleed or smudge, and although it does wash out with repeated laundering, it simply fades out without running onto the face and can be easily replaced when the doll is dry.

To make round, rosy cheeks, take a scrap of fabric and scribble a solid patch of colour in the centre of it. Place fabric over your index finger and rub colour onto face with a circular motion. Use sparingly at first – you can always repeat the procedure if the colour is too light. A white tissue will remove excess colour.

Three-dimensional dolls look better if the eyes are slightly sunk into the head, as though they were in sockets.

To do this, use a long thin needle with a suitable coloured strong thread.

Anchor the thread with a knot

or couple of stitches on the side of the head behind the hairline.

Insert the needle through the head and into the eye, then take a tiny stitch and return to starting point, pulling the thread slightly.

Fasten off securely.

Remember to check that both eyes are symmetrical after this procedure. If white thread is used, the sculpture stitch can double as a highlight.

Either white paint or white thread can be used for highlights, but whichever you use, make sure that the highlights are on the same side for both eyes and are the same size.

Age and sex differences

The basic difference between adult and child faces is the length of the face and the position of the features.

Adult: eyes on halfway line, longer nose than child.

Child: rounder face, lower eyes, eyes spaced wider apart, shorter nose.

Male faces: heavier eyebrows, larger or heavier line for nose, squarer chin, narrower lips in brownish pink rather than pink or red, omit eyelashes and eyeshadow.

Eyes

The easiest eyes are simple spots or circles. Beware of placing them too close together, or the doll will look mean or cross-eyed.

In general, eyes should be the width of one eye apart, with children's eyes being more widely spaced than those of adults.

Make sure the spots or circles are level and the same size. Don't rely on glue for attaching felt circles – stitching is much more secure.

Add white highlights for an alert, lively expression. Add eyelashes and eyebrows, if desired.

If your doll is large or sophisticated in appearance, you will need more detailed eyes. In small dolls, there is probably no need to draw the pupil – just paint or embroider the iris in a solid colour. For larger dolls, a black pupil can be added.

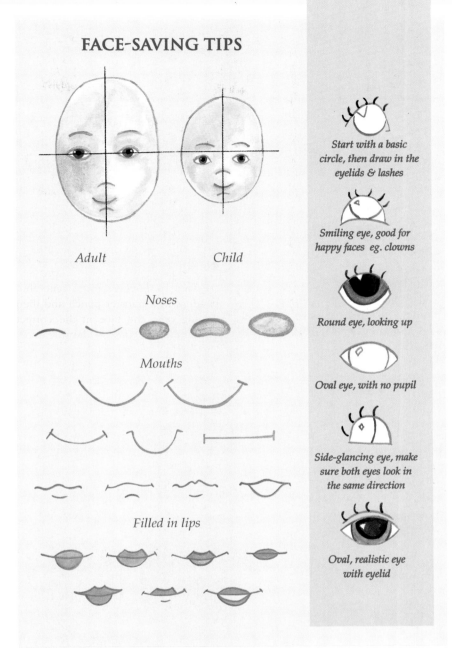

FACE-SAVING TIPS

Adult   Child

Noses

Mouths

Filled in lips

Start with a basic circle, then draw in the eyelids & lashes

Smiling eye, good for happy faces eg. clowns

Round eye, looking up

Oval eye, with no pupil

Side-glancing eye, make sure both eyes look in the same direction

Oval, realistic eye with eyelid

Noses

A slightly darker than flesh colour is most suitable for noses. The nose can be represented by an outline only, or the shape can be filled in with satin-stitch.

Padded satin-stitch can be used for filled-in types, to give them an extra dimension.

Mouths

These range from the very simple curved or straight line to shaped lips. For simple faces, a curved line is probably most appropriate. A coin can be used as an outline to obtain an even curve.

"Smile" lines can be added and the expression varied by the depth of the curve.

On soft sculpture dolls, the mouth is generally indicated by a long stitch, pulled tight to indent it.

For child dolls, avoid a dark or bright red, as it looks harsh and unnatural. Any shade of pink or orange is more suitable.

On more detailed dolls, a more elaborate mouth is more appropriate.

BLACK MAMMY DOLL

Measurements

The finished doll measures approximately 44cm tall.

Materials

- ◾ One pair brown cotton socks, men's shoe size 6-10
- ◾ Polyester filling
- ◾ Black wool (we used a nylon/acrylic "mohair")
- ◾ Two small black shank-style buttons, for Eyes
- ◾ Two brass or gold "rings", for earrings
- ◾ Tiny scrap red felt
- ◾ 0.4m x 90cm cheesecloth
- ◾ 0.3m x 90cm red flannelette
- ◾ 0.25m x 115cm small print, for Dress
- ◾ 0.3m x 90cm calico
- ◾ 0.25m x 90cm striped or spotted fabric, for Bandanna
- ◾ Red bias binding (optional)
- ◾ 1.2m x 3cm-wide écru cotton lace edging
- ◾ 0.25m x 3mm-wide elastic
- ◾ Six x 1cm-diameter buttons
- ◾ Nine small press-studs
- ◾ Small amount cream perle cotton (or similar)
- ◾ Small safety pin

Pattern pieces

There are no pattern pieces for the Doll, as she is constructed from socks, following diagrams, right and overleaf. All pattern pieces for Doll's Clothes, except the rectangles, are printed on the pattern sheet, Side 3, in red. Trace Bloomers Front/Back 1, Camisole Front 2, Camisole Back 3, Petticoat Front/Dress Back Bodice 4, Petticoat Back/Dress Front Bodice 5, Skirt Front/Back 6 and Sleeve 7.

Cutting

Note. A 6mm seam allowance is *included* on all pattern pieces unless it is otherwise indicated.

From cheesecloth, cut two Bloomers Front/Backs, one Camisole Front and two Camisole Backs.

From red flannelette, cut one Petticoat Front Bodice, two Petticoat Back Bodices and one Skirt (cutting to Petticoat length).

If not using purchased bias binding, cut also enough bias strips to bind neck and armholes.

From small print, cut two Dress Front Bodices, one Dress Back Bodice, one Skirt (cutting to Dress length) and two Sleeves.

Diagram 1. Diagram 2.

Cut also a narrow bias strip for finishing the neck edge.

From the calico, cut one rectangle, 45cm x 21cm, for the Apron Skirt, and a strip, 78cm x 5cm, for the Apron Waistband/Ties.

From the striped fabric, cut two rectangles, each 60cm x 12cm, for Bandanna.

Sewing

DOLL

Take one brown sock and push some polyester filling into the toe, a little at a time, gradually building up a rounded head shape, turning the sock and rearranging the stuffing as necessary to achieve a smooth shape. Choose the smooth side of the sock, without the toe seam, for the face, and mould your stuffing on this side so that the face looks symmetrical. When the head is about the size of a small grapefruit, add a little extra stuffing to create a neck area, then run a double gathering thread around the neck, draw up the thread and knot it off securely. Trim away excess sock fabric, leaving about 1.5cm below the gathering thread. Reserve excess fabric for Arms.

Lay the second brown sock so that the instep faces upwards, with the heel centred underneath (see *Diagram 1, left*). Fold the heel towards the upper edge of the sock.

Cut up the centre of the sock, from the toe edge almost to the heel. Turn sock wrong side out.

Following *Diagram 2*, and stitching about 4mm from the raw edges, sew the leg seams on the sock, rounding the first foot, stitching up one leg, across the crotch, down the other leg and rounding the second foot. Trim the excess fabric from foot seams and turn the right side out.

Stuff each foot for about 5cm, then

THAT OLD BLACK MAGIC

An old-fashioned Mammy doll is sure to become a much-loved bedtime companion – and who'd ever guess that she started life as a pair of brown cotton socks? With soft, crinkly black hair, big gold earrings, colourful bandanna and lots of layers of clothes, including a wonderful flannelette petticoat (her pride and joy), this Mammy is a delightful interpretation of a traditional favourite.

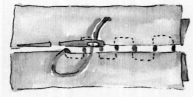

Diagram 3.

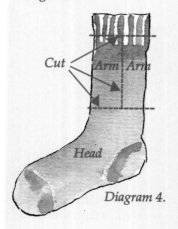

Diagram 4.

run a pin across each leg above the stuffing and continue to stuff legs, leaving a slight gap at the top so that legs will swing freely when doll is complete. When legs are stuffed, remove pins and bend foot up towards leg (so that foot is at right angles to leg). Using brown thread and holding foot in position, ladder-stitch (see **Diagram 3**) along the crease between foot and leg, pulling thread firmly to hold foot in position. Stitch back along the seam for extra firmness, then secure thread and bury ends.

Use a large piece of stuffing to create the doll's bottom in the heel of the sock, then continue stuffing body until it is a length proportionate to legs and size of head. Run a gathering thread around the top of the torso and draw up thread, pushing stuffing towards the shoulders as you do so to create a slight "seat" for the head.

Press the head onto the body and, using double thread, ladder stitch around the neck, tucking the raw edges to the inside as you stitch and .drawing up thread firmly to keep the head in place. If the head seems to be too floppy as you stitch, poke a little extra stuffing into the neck before closing the seam, but remember that there is no real "neck" on this doll – the head should sit firmly on the torso. Stitch twice around the neck to create

a strong seam, then knot off thread securely at the back and bury ends.

From the excess fabric that you reserved from the Head, cut the Arms, as shown in **Diagram 4**. Refold each piece so that the right sides are together and stitch along the seam opposite the fold and around one end, creating a rounded tube. Turn right side out and stuff, noting that you can adjust the length with more or less stuffing. Leave 4cm at the top of each Arm unstuffed. Turn in raw edges on each Arm and stitch Arms firmly to Body so that arm seam runs on the underside of the Arm and the top opening is flattened against the shoulder. The unstuffed segment at the top of each Arm allows the Arm to be moved in any direction for playing and dressing. To create hands, run a double gathering thread around each Arm, about 2.5cm from finished end, draw up thread to create a wrist, knot off firmly and bury ends.

To make curly hair, wrap black wool around the handle of a large wooden spoon, from one end to the other. Thread extending end onto a needle and back-stitch along the length of the coils (see **Diagram 5**), picking up each coil as you stitch. Tie off the end, then gently slip yarn coils off the spoon handle, taking care not to twist them. Using black sewing thread and starting in the centre back of the doll's head, stitch the coils to the head, stitching through the backstitch holding row and working outwards in a spiral from centre point. Keep working in this manner, creating and adding more coils until doll has a full head of tightly curled hair. If you wish to make hair longer at the back than the front, add a couple of straight rows below the spiral, at the sides and back only (see **Diagram 6**).

Stitch small black buttons to doll's face for eyes and stitch gold rings to either side of head for earrings. Cut a small heart shape from red felt and stitch in place for mouth.

CLOTHES

Bloomers: With right sides together, stitch centre front and back seams of

Bloomers Front/Backs. With right sides together, stitch inner leg seam.

Edge-finish waist edge with over-locking or zigzag. Press 1cm to inside and stitch close to finished edge.

Press 1cm on leg edges to **outside** and zigzag in place along raw edge. Cut cotton lace to fit leg edges (plus turnings) and stitch in place, positioning upper edge of lace over the zigzag stitching. Turn in raw ends of lace and finish by hand.

Make a twisted cord from two strands of perle thread. Thread a large needle (such as a tapestry needle) with the twisted cord and, starting on one side of centre front seam, thread twisted cord through waist casing, emerging back at centre front seam. Knot ends of cord. Place Bloomers on doll, draw up waist cord to fit and tie in a bow.

Camisole: With right sides together, stitch Front to Backs at shoulder seams. Press a tiny hem on armhole and neck edges and top-stitch in place.

With right sides together, stitch Front to Backs at side seams.

Edge-finish lower raw edge, press up seam allowance and top-stitch hem in place. Follow the same procedure for back opening edges, noting that 1.5cm seams are allowed on opening edges.

Cut a piece of cotton lace to fit hem edge, plus turnings, and top-stitch to lower edge, turning in and neatening raw ends at opening edges.

Using a tapestry needle, thread a single strand of perle thread through the turning at neck edge; knot ends. Place Camisole on doll, pull up neck drawstring to fit and tie in a bow at back neck.

Petticoat: With right sides together, stitch Front Bodice to Back Bodices at shoulders and side seams.

With purchased or self-made bias binding, finish armholes and neck edge, and top-stitch close to finished edges, if desired. Alternatively, edge-finish the armholes and neck edge, press seam allowance to inside, clipping curves where necessary, and top-stitch in place.

With right sides together, stitch centre back seam of Skirt, in a 1.5cm

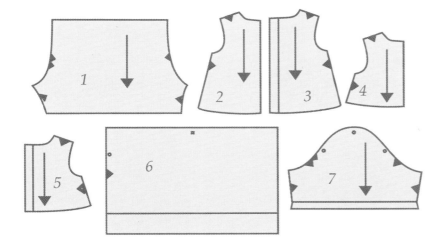

outside, sew six small buttons over press-stud positions.

Apron: Finish the short edges and one long edge of the Apron Skirt with a narrow hem. Mark the centre point of the remaining raw edge of Skirt, then run a gathering thread along the edge.

Fold Waistband/tie rectangle in half crosswise and mark centre point. With right sides together, raw edges even and centre points matching, pin Skirt to Waistband and draw up Skirt so that upper edge measures approximately 16cm, that is, 8cm on either side of centre point. Stitch. Fold Waistband in half, right sides together, and stitch tie seams, starting each seam close to Skirt and finishing by stitching across short end of each tie. Trim corners. Turn Waistband/Ties right side out, press under remaining raw edge on the Waistband and slip-stitch in place over the seam.

Bandanna: With right sides facing, stitch Bandanna rectangles together around all edges, leaving an opening for turning. Turn right side out, press and slip-stitch opening edges together. Place Bandanna around Doll's head and tie in front. To avoid a second bulky knot, arrange ends in desired position and secure at the back with a small safety pin or a stitch.

seam, pivoting at small dot and stitching across seam allowance. Leave seam open above small dot. Clip to stitching at small dot and press seam open. Run a gathering thread around waist edge of Skirt and draw up gathers to fit Bodice. With right sides together, stitch Skirt to Bodice. Trim seam, press seam towards Bodice and top-stitch close to seam. Edge-finish Back opening edges above small dot. Press under 1.5cm seam allowance on lefthand opening edge and catch in place at neck edge and waist edge. Lap left Back over right Back and sew on three press-studs to secure opening.

Finish hem on lower edge by hand or machine.

Dress: With right sides together, stitch Back Bodice to Front Bodices at the shoulder seams.

Edge-finish lower edge of Sleeves, press under seam allowance and stitch close to finished edge, creating a casing. Cut two pieces of elastic and thread through casing. Stitch across one end to secure, then pull up elastic to desired width of Sleeve (test around doll's arm) and stitch across second end to secure. Trim excess elastic.

Run a gathering thread around crown of Sleeve and draw up gathers to fit armholes. With right sides together, stitch Sleeves to armholes. Trim and neaten seams. With right sides together, stitch Sleeve and side seams in one continuous operation, matching the armhole seams.

With right sides together, stitch bias strip to neck edge of Bodice, fold bias to inside, press under raw edge on bias and slip-stitch in place, avoiding the stitches showing on the outside.

Run a gathering thread around upper edge of Skirt and draw up gathers to fit Bodice. With right sides together, stitch Skirt to Bodice. Trim and neaten seam and press towards Bodice. Edge-finish opening edges of Dress, from neck edge to lower edge.

Finish hem on lower edge by hand or machine.

Press under 1.5cm seam allowance on lefthand opening edge and secure in place at neck, waist and hem edges. Lap left Front over right Front and sew on six press-studs at evenly spaced intervals to secure Front opening. On

Diagram 5.

Diagram 6.

KNITTED DOLL

Measurements

Approximately 45cm high.

Materials

Milford Soft 4-ply (50g):
■ 2 balls unbleached
■ Small quantities of pink, white, lavender, pale yellow and pink-red
■ One pair of 2.75mm (No 12) knitting needles
■ One 2.50mm crochet hook
■ Polyester fibre filling
■ Tapestry needle or knitter's needle for sewing seams and embroidery

Tension: See **Knitting and Crochet Notes** on page 120.

30 sts and 41 rows to 10cm over st st, using 2.75mm needles.

Special abbreviation

M1: Make one st (pick up strand between st just worked and next st, place it on left-hand needle and knit into back).

Leg (make 2)

1st row (wrong side). Purl.
Break off pink yarn; join in unbleached yarn.
Work 30 rows st st, beg with a knit row.

Shape knee. 32nd row. K11, sl 1, K1, psso, K3, K2tog, K11…27 sts.

33rd row. Purl.

34th row. K11, sl 1, K1, psso, K1, K2tog, K11…25 sts.
Work 5 rows st st, beg with a purl row.

40th row. K3, M1, K19, M1, K3…27 sts.

41st row. Purl.

42nd row. K3, M1, K21, M1, K3…29 sts.
Work 7 rows st st, beg with a purl row.

50th row. K2, sl 1, K1, psso, K21, K2tog, K2…27 sts.

Work 3 rows st st, beg with a purl row.

54th row. K2, sl 1, K1, psso, K19, K2tog, K2…25 sts.

55th row. Purl.

56th row. K2, sl 1, K1, psso, K17, K2tog, K2…23 sts.
Break off unbleached yarn. Join in white yarn for sock top.

57th row. Purl.

58th row. P2, P2tog, P15, P2tog, P2…21 sts.

59th row. Purl.

60th row. K2, sl 1, K1, psso, K13, K2tog, K2…19 sts.
Break off white yarn. Join in lavender yarn for shoe.

61st row. Purl.

Shape heel. Next row. K7, *turn.*
Cont on these 7 sts only, work 5 rows st st, beg with a purl row.

Next row. K4, *turn,* sl 1, P3, *turn,* K5, *turn,* sl 1, P4, *turn,* K6, *turn,* sl 1, P5, *turn,* K7. Break off yarn.
With right side facing, sl next 5 sts on right-hand needle so there are 12 sts on right-hand needle. Join lavender yarn to rem 7 sts on left-hand needle and knit to end.
Cont on last 7 sts only, work 4 rows st st, beg with a purl row.

Next row. P4, *turn,* sl 1, K3, *turn,* P5, *turn,* sl 1, K4, *turn,* P6, *turn,* sl 1, K5, *turn,* P7, *turn,* sl 1, K6.

Join shoe pieces by working across all sts as folls.

1st row (wrong side). P7, knit up 3 sts along side edge of heel, P5, knit up 3 sts along other side edge of heel, P7…25 sts.

2nd row. K8, K2tog, K5, sl 1, K1, psso, K8…23 sts.

3rd row. Purl.

4th row. K7, K2tog, K5, sl 1, K1, psso, K7…21 sts.

5th row. Purl.

6th row. K6, K2tog, K5, sl 1, K1, psso, K6…19 sts.
Work 3 rows st st, beg with a purl row.

10th row. K5, K2tog, K5, sl 1, K1, psso, K5…17 sts.

11th row. Purl.

12th row. K4, K2tog, K5, sl 1, K1, psso, K4…15 sts.

13th row. Purl.

14th row. K3, K2tog, K5, sl 1, K1, psso, K3…13 sts.

15th row. Purl.
Break off yarn leaving a long end. Lace a separate length of yarn through rem sts, pull tight and knot ends tog.

Arm (make 2)

Using unbleached yarn and 2.75mm needles, cast on 18 sts for top edge.

1st row (wrong side). Purl.
Work 2 rows st st, beg with a knit row.

4th row. K3, M1, K12, M1, K3…20 sts.
Work 3 rows st st, beg with a purl row.

8th row. K3, M1, K14, M1, K3…22 sts.
Work 3 rows st st, beg with a purl row.

12th row. K3, M1, K16, M1, K3…24 sts.
Work 15 rows st st, beg with a purl row.

28th row. K9, K2tog, K2, sl 1, K1, psso, K9…22 sts.
Work 3 rows st st, beg with a purl row.

32nd row. K9, M1, K4, M1, K9…24 sts.
Work 7 rows st st, beg with a purl row.

40th row. K2, sl 1, K1, psso, K16, K2tog, K2…22 sts.
Work 3 rows st st, beg with a purl row.

44th row. K2, sl 1, K1, psso, K14, K2tog, K2…20 sts.
Work 3 rows st st, beg with a purl row.

48th row. K2, sl 1, K1, psso, K12, K2tog, K2…18 sts.
Work 3 rows st st, beg with a purl row.

KNIT LOVABLE EMILY

Meet Emily, who is especially cute and ever so cuddly. Knitted in soft cotton and dressed to charm, Emily is sure to become one of those special toys that are loved to near shabbiness. It's then her washability will be prized as well. Emily's knickers and socks are knitted as part of the body. Her outer clothes, dress, petticoat and apron with lace trim and ties, will suit any similarly sized doll.

52nd row. K2, sl 1, K1, psso, K10, K2tog, K2...16 sts.

Work 3 rows st st, beg with a purl row.

56th row. K2, sl 1, K1, psso, K8, K2tog, K2...14 sts.

Work 3 rows st st, beg with a purl row, for wrist.

Shape thumb. 60th row. K1, M1, K5, M1, K2, M1, K5, M1, K1...18 sts.

61st and alt rows. Purl.

62nd row. K8, M1, K2, M1, K8...20 sts.

64th row. K8, M1, K4, M1, K8...22 sts.

66th row. K8, M1, K6, M1, K8...24 sts.

68th row. K10, K2tog, sl 1, K1, psso, K10...22 sts.

69th row. P9, P2tog tbl, P2tog, P9...20 sts.

70th row. K8, K2tog, sl 1, K1, psso, K8...18 sts.

71st row. P7, P2tog tbl, P2tog, P7...16 sts.

Work 5 rows st st, beg with a knit row.

77th row. (K2tog) 8 times...8 sts. Break off yarn, leaving a long end. Lace a separate length of yarn through rem sts, pull tight and knot ends tog.

Body

Using pink yarn, cast on 56 sts for lower edge.

1st row (wrong side). Purl.

Change to white yarn.

2nd row. Knit.

3rd row. Purl.

Change to pink yarn.

4th row. Knit, inc 6 sts evenly across row....62 sts.

5th row. Purl.

Change to white yarn.

6th row. K16, M1, K30, M1, K16...64 sts.

7th row. Purl.

Change to pink yarn.

8th row. K16, M1, K32, M1, K16...66 sts.

9th row. Purl.

Change to white yarn.

10th row. K17, M1, K32, M1, K17...68 sts.

11th row. Purl.

Work a further 6 rows st st in stripes of 2 rows pink yarn, 2 rows white yarn, then 2 rows pink yarn.

Change to unbleached yarn for rem. Work a further 6 rows st st.

24th row. K16, sl 1, K1, psso, K32, K2tog, K16...66 sts.

25th and alt rows. Purl.

26th row. K15, K2tog, sl 1, K1, psso, K28, K2tog, sl 1, K1, psso, K15...62 sts.

28th row. K1, sl 1, K1, psso, K11, K2tog, sl 1, K1, psso, K11, (P2tog) twice for navel, K11, K2tog, sl 1, K1, psso, K11, K2tog, K1...54 sts.

30th row. K1, sl 1, K1, psso, K48, K2tog, K1...52 sts.

Work 5 rows st st, beg with a purl row, for waist.

36th row. K13, M1, K26, M1, K13...54 sts.

Work 3 rows st st, beg with a purl row.

40th row. K14, M1, K26, M1, K14...56 sts.

Work 3 rows st st, beg with a purl row.

44th row. K14, M1, K28, M1, K14...58 sts.

Work 3 rows st st, beg with a purl row.

48th row. K15, M1, K28, M1, K15...60 sts.

Work 11 rows st st, beg with a purl row.

60th row. K14, sl 1, K2tog, psso, K26, sl 1, K2tog, psso, K14...56 sts.

61st row. Purl.

62nd row. Shape shoulders. K8, *cast off next 13 sts noting to knit tog the 5th and 6th sts and the 8th and 9th sts before casting-off*, knit until there are 14 sts on right-hand needle for Front neck, work as from * to *, knit to end...30 sts.

63rd row. P7, P2tog, P12, P2tog, P7...28 sts.

Work 3 rows st st, beg with a knit row.

Cast off purlways.

Head

Using unbleached yarn and 2.75mm needles, cast on 28 sts for lower edge.

1st row (wrong side). Purl.

Work 4 rows st st, beg with a knit row.

6th row. Knit into front and then into back of each st...56 sts.

Work 3 rows st st, beg with a purl row.

10th row. K14, M1, K1, M1, K26, M1, K1, M1, K14...60 sts.

11th row. Purl.

12th row. K14, M1, K3, M1, K26, M1, K3, M1, K14...64 sts.

Work 3 rows st st, beg with a purl row.

16th row. K15, M1, K3, M1, K28, M1, K3, M1, K15...68 sts.

Work 3 rows st st, beg with a purl row.

20th row. K16, M1, K3, M1, K30, M1, K3, M1, K16...72 sts.

Work 5 rows st st, beg with a purl row.

26th row. K35, P2tog for nose, K35...71 sts.

Work 5 rows st st, beg with a purl row.

32nd row. K15, sl 1, K1, psso, K3, K2tog, K27, sl 1, K1, psso, K3, K2tog, K15...67 sts.

Work 3 rows st st, beg with a purl row.

36th row. K14, sl 1, K1, psso, K3, K2tog, K25, sl 1, K1, psso, K3, K2tog, K14...63 sts.

Work 3 rows st st, beg with a purl row.

40th row. K13, sl 1, K1, psso, K3, K2tog, K23, sl 1, K1, psso, K3, K2tog, K13...59 sts.

Work 3 rows st st, beg with a purl row.

44th row. K12, sl 1, K1, psso, K3, K2tog, K21, sl 1, K1, psso, K3, K2tog, K12...55 sts.

Work 3 rows st st, beg with a purl row.

48th row. *K2, K2tog; rep from * to last 3 sts, K3...42 sts.

49th and alt rows. Purl.

50th row. *K1, K2tog; rep from * to end...28 sts.

52nd row. (K2tog) to end...14 sts.

53rd row. Purl.

Break off yarn, leaving a long end. Lace a separate length of yarn through rem sts, pull tight and knot ends tog.

To make up

Close centre back seam and lower edge seam of Body. Close shoulder seams. Fill firmly, leaving neck edge open. Using white yarn, embroider white area of socks in knitting-stitch as folls: start on the 5th blue row from the sock and embroider over the 3 centre sts of the upper foot, working 4 rows in height. Close sole of shoes and back seam of socks. Fill firmly and close rem of back seam of Legs. Fill Legs and close top edge in such a way that the seam will lie at the back. Sew Legs to lower edge of Body, with shoes pointing forwards.

For Arms, first close hand seams and fill. Close rem of Arms, leaving top edge open, and fill. Close top edge of

1. The panties form part of the body section.

2. Stitch the body leaving an opening for filling.

3. After sewing the seam, close the top and bottom of the head with running stitches.

4. The features are embroidered with knitting stitch, and Emily's hair is knotted on.

5. The legs with socks and shoes are knitted in one piece.

6. To shape the arms, decrease or add a few stitches.

7. Combine a plain dress with a flowered pinny, or a plain pinny with a floral sprig dress.

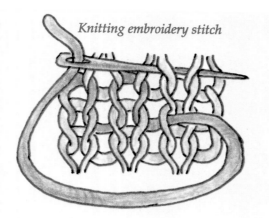

Knitting embroidery stitch

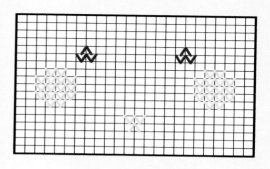

Graph for face

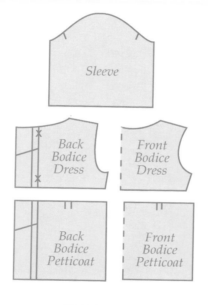

Arms in such a way that the seam will lie on top of the Arm with thumbs positioned correctly. Sew Arms to shoulders. Top-stitch a small area of the thumb. Foll diagram, embroider features with half and full knitting-stitches. Work mouth with pink-red, cheeks with pink, eyes with lavender.

Note: On the graph, the nose is marked over 2 sts, but because of the P2tog sts for the nose, only one st rems above the nose. Because of this there are only 7 sts instead of 8 sts between the eyes.

Close the back Head seam. Fill Head firmly. Work a row of running-stitch through the cast-on row, pull tight and knot ends tog. Fill neck a bit more and sew Head to Body. The 5th row of the Head (the row *before* the inc) will lie against the cast-off row of the neck).

For the hair, cut 65cm-long lengths of pale yellow yarn and knot these onto top of Head as folls. Fold each length in half, then using crochet hook, pull fold through one knitted st then bring ends over top of st and through fold (loop); pull tight.

Work lengths as folls. For Front Head, in the 11th row above the eyes and over 13 sts in width.

Back Head: in the 10th row above neck and over 18 sts in width.

Sides: knot the hair in a diagonal line from the Front Head towards the Back Head. Tie the hair tog on top of the Head in a pony tail. Trim hair if needed. Cut a few short pieces of yarn for the fringe and sides of the head. Knot these at the top side of the face and at ear-level against the hairline.

DRESS

Materials

- 0.35m of 90cm wide floral or plain cotton
- 65cm of 2cm wide white lace for Floral Dress; 35cm for Plain Dress
- 2 press-studs
- 16cm of 3mm elastic

Pattern pieces

All pattern pieces are printed in a separate panel on the pattern sheet, Side 4, in black. Trace Bodice Front, Bodice Back and Sleeve.

Cutting

Note. *Add* a 1cm seam allowance to all pattern pieces, except the neck edges of Bodice pieces.

From cotton, cut one Bodice Front, two Bodice Backs, two Sleeves, one rectangle 90cm x 16cm for Skirt and one bias strip 18cm x 2.5cm for Neck Band.

Sewing

With right sides together, sew Bodice Front to Bodice Backs at shoulder seams and the Neck Band to the neck edge, allowing a 0.5cm seam. Fold the band inwards over the seam and topstitch.

Press the seam allowance on the lower edge of the Sleeves inwards. Place the lower edge of the Sleeves on top of a piece of lace, and sew together with zigzag stitch. Carefully cut away surplus seam close to the lace. Zigzag an 8cm piece of elastic, slightly stretched, to the inside sleeves. Position the elastic 0.5cm above lace.

With right sides together, gather the top of sleeves between the symbols and sew sleeves to the bodice.

Sew the side and sleeve seams in one continuous seam.

With right sides together, stitch the centre-back seam of Skirt, leaving a 7cm opening at the top. Press the opening seams flat. Gather the top edge of skirt.

With right sides together and back bodice facings turned outwards, pin the skirt to the bodice from centre back to centre back. Stitch in place and turn the facings.

Turn up and stitch a 2cm wide hem on the lower edge of skirt. Sew the press-studs to the back bodice.

On *Floral Dress,* make a narrow hem in the short sides of the remaining piece of lace. Gather the top edge of the lace with small running stitches. Sew in place closely below the neck band, from the centre back to the centre back. Secure the back bodice facings at the top with small stitches.

On **Plain Dress,** omit this step.

PETTICOAT

Materials

- ◼ 0.20m x 90cm white cotton
- ◼ 1.30m x 2cm white lace
- ◼ 25cm white bias binding
- ◼ 2 small pieces white velcro

Pattern pieces

All pattern pieces are printed in a separate panel on the pattern sheet, Side 4, in black. Trace Petticoat Front Bodice and Petticoat Back Bodice.

Cutting

Note. Cut all fabric pieces *adding* 1cm seam allowance.

From fabric, cut one Front Bodice, one Back Bodice and a rectangle 90cm x 10cm for the Skirt.

Sewing

With right sides together, stitch Bodice sides. Press under seam at top edge of the bodice. Zigzag the top edge onto a piece of lace.

Press under 1cm wide seam at the lower edge of the skirt. Zigzag the lower edge of the skirt onto a piece of lace. With right sides together, stitch the centre-back seam of the skirt, leaving a 5cm opening at the top. Press the seams of the opening flat. Gather the top edge of the skirt. With right sides together and back facings turned outwards, pin the skirt to the bodice from centre-back to centre-back. Stitch and turn the facings right side out.

Fold bias binding in half lengthwise and stitch. Cut in half to make two thin shoulder straps. Secure ends to the inside of the bodice, where indicated. Sew the velcro to back facings.

APRON

Materials

- ◼ 0.15cm x 90cm wide white floral cotton
- ◼ 2m x 1cm white lace

Cutting

Cut one 60cm x 12cm rectangle for Skirt, one 30cm x 5cm strip for Waistband and one 10cm x 8cm rectangle for Bib.

These sizes *include* a 1cm seam allowance.

Sewing

Press under 1cm along short edges and 1cm along one long edge of Skirt. Zigzag lace to the sides and lower edge of the skirt and trim close to stitching. Gather the top edge of the skirt to 20cm.

With centres matched, sew the skirt to one long side of the waistband.

Fold the waistband in half lengthwise, wrong side out and stitch both short ends.

Trim seam corners diagonally, turn right side out, and slip-stitch the band inside the skirt.

To form a loop for the ties, fold under 2cm at each end of the waistband, and stitch it in place. Bringing right sides together, fold the bib in half, making it 5cm x 8cm, and stitch across short edges. Cut off seam corners diagonally and turn the bib right side out.

Cut a 7cm piece of lace. Zigzag the top edge of the bib to this piece of lace, allowing 0.5cm to extend at each side.

Cut the remaining lace in half and pin to each side of the bib, with raw edges even at lower side.

Zigzag the lace in place on both sides, also sewing over the extending 0.5cm lace at the top of the bib.

The unstitched tails of lace form the apron ties. Slip-stitch the top edge of the waistband to the bib, with centres matching.

ONCE A JOLLY SWAGMAN

Measurements

Approximately 40cm high.

Abbreviations: See Knitting and Crochet Notes, page 120.

Materials

8-ply yarn:
- 25g grey for Trousers
- 25g light brown for Trousers
- 50g grey for Hat
- 25g green for Boots and Belt
- 25g blue for Top
- 75g navy for Coat
- Small amount maroon for Scarf
- 50g white for Head and Hands (see **Note**)
- 25g rust for Bed-Roll and Buckle
- Ball of brown wool, for Hair (we used a synthetic "mohair")
- One pair of 3mm (No 11) knitting needles
- One 3mm crochet hook
- Black felt for eyes
- Polyester fibre filling
- Small cardboard spice container
- Craft glue
- Coat-hanger wire
- Black paint
- Tapestry needle
- Paintbrush
- PVA glue
- Corks
- Two buttons for Coat
- Pink embroidery thread
- Blusher or red pencil
- One cup-sized teabag
- White, yellow and grey polymer clay, for Cockatoo

Note: Dye knitted Head and Hand pieces in a weak solution of tea as follows. Bring two litres of water to boil, add one tea bag, then add knitted pieces and simmer for 15 minutes. Remove pieces with tongs, rinse under cold running water for 5 minutes (until yarn cools down). Return pieces to tea solution, simmer for a further five minutes. Rinse under cold running water, wrap up in a towel and squeeze out water. Leave pieces to dry on flat surface.

Boots (make 2)

Using green yarn, cast on 50 sts.
Work 6 rows st st.
7th row. K23, (K2tog) twice, knit to end...48sts.
8th and foll alt rows. Purl.
9th row. K22, (K2tog) twice, knit to end...46sts.
11th row. K21, (K2tog) twice, knit to end...44sts.
13th row. K20, (K2tog) twice, knit to end...42sts.
15th row. K15, cast off next 12 sts, knit to end.
16th row. Purl across all 30 sts. Work 4 rows st st.
Cast off.

Soles (make 2)

Using green yarn, cast on 8 sts.
1st row. Knit.
2nd row. Purl, inc one st at each end.
Rep last 2 rows until there are 16 sts.
Work 9 rows st st, thus ending with a knit row.
Dec one st at each end of next and foll alt rows until 10 sts rem.
Next row. Knit.
Next row. P4, P2tog, P4...9 sts.
Cast off.

Trousers
(worked sideways)

Right Back Leg
Using light brown, cast on 40 sts.
1st row (right side). Purl.
2nd row. Knit.
Rep last 2 rows 7 times more in stripes of 2 rows grey and 2 rows light brown.

Keeping stripes correct, shape Leg as folls.**
17th row and foll alt rows. Purl.
18th row. Cast off 16 sts, knit to end...24 sts.
20th row. K2tog, knit to end...23 sts.
22nd row. K2tog, knit to end...22 sts.
23rd row. Purl. Cast off.
Work another piece for *Left Front Leg.*

Left Back Leg
Work as for Right Back Leg to **.
17th row. Cast off 16 sts, purl to end...24 sts.
18th and foll alt rows. Knit.
19th row. P2tog, purl to end...23 sts.
21st row. P2tog, purl to end...22 sts.
23rd row. Purl. Cast off.
Knit another piece for *Right Front Leg.*

Top (make 2)

Using blue yarn, cast on 30 sts.
Work 26 rows st st.
Shape top. Cont in st st, cast off 4 sts at beg of next 4 rows...14 sts.
Work 4 rows st st.
Cast off.

Sleeve (make 2)

Using blue yarn, cast on 25 sts.
Work 30 rows st st.
Shape top. Cont in st st, cast off 4 sts at beg of next 4 rows...9 sts.
Cast off.

Belt

Using green yarn, cast on 70 sts.
Work 4 rows st st.
Cast off.

Buckle

Using rust yarn, cast on 6 sts.
1st row. Knit.
2nd row. P2, cast off 2 sts, P1...4sts.
3rd row. K2, cast on 2 sts, K2.
4th row. Purl.
Cast off.

ONCE A JOLLY SWAGMAN

And here he is! The very fellow who camped by a billabong and sang while his billy boiled, brought to life. Our Australian swagman is knitted in easy sections and is perfect in every detail, from his cork-trimmed hat and rolled swag, to his fire-blackened billy, complete with tame cockatoo. Here is a toy that will immediately delight all children.

Coat

Left Front

Using navy yarn, cast on 17 sts.
1st row. K1, *P1, K1; rep from * to end.
Last row forms moss st patt.
Rep last row 45 times more.***
Shape shoulder. 47th row. Cast off 4 sts, moss st to end.
48th row. Work in moss st.
Rep last 2 rows once more...9 sts.
Cast off.

Right Front

Work as for Left Front to ***.
Work one row moss st.
Shape shoulder. 48th row. Cast off 4 sts, moss st to end.
49th row. Work in moss st.

Rep last 2 rows once more...9 sts.
Cast off.

Back

Using navy yarn, cast on 34 sts.
1st row. *K1, P1; rep from * to end.
2nd row. *Pl, K1; rep from * to end.
Last 2 rows form moss st patt.
Rep last 2 rows 22 times more...46 rows in all.
Shape shoulders. Cont in moss st, cast off 4 sts at beg of next 4 rows...18 sts. Cast off.

Sleeve (make 2)

Using navy yarn, cast on 25 sts.
Working in moss st as for Fronts, work 28 rows.
Cont in moss st, dec one st at beg of every row until 10 sts rem.
Cast off.

Hands (make 2)

Knit with white yarn, then dye in tea solution (see **Note** page 38).
Using white yarn, cast on 25 sts.
Work 6 rows st st.
Cont in st st for rem, inc one st at beg of next 4 rows...29 sts.
Dec one st at beg of next 2 rows...27 sts.
Cast off 3 sts at beg of next 2 rows...21 sts.
Dec one st at beg of next row.
Next row. P2tog, P8, P2tog, P8...18 sts.
Work 2 rows st st.
Next row. (K2tog) to end...9 sts.
Next row. Purl.
Cast off.

Head (make 2)

Knit with white yarn, then dye in tea solution (see **Note** page 38).
Using white yarn, cast on 12 sts.
1st row. Knit.
2nd row. Purl.
3rd row. Knit, inc one st in each st...24 sts.
4th row. Purl.
Cont in st st, inc one st at beg of every row until there are 30 sts.
Work 28 rows st st.
Next row. *K1, K2tog; rep from* to end...20 sts.

Next row. Purl.
Next row. (K2tog) to end...10 sts.
Cast off.

Hat

Crown

Using grey yarn, cast on 66 sts.
Work 26 rows garter st.
27th row. *K4, K2tog; rep from* to end...55 sts.
28th and foll alt rows. Knit.
29th row. *K3, K2tog; rep from * to end...44 sts.
31st row. *K2, K2tog; rep from * to end...33 sts.
33rd row. *K1, K2tog; rep from * to end...22 sts.
34th row. (K2tog) to end...11 sts.
35th row. (K2tog) to last st, K1...6 sts.
Break off yarn, thread end through rem sts, draw up and fasten off securely.

Brim

Using grey yarn, cast on 132 sts.
Work 15 rows garter st.
16th row. *K4, K2tog; rep from * to end...110 sts.
17th row. Knit.
18th row. *K1, K2tog; rep from * to last 2 sts, K2...74 sts.
19th row. Knit.
Cast off.

Scarf

Using maroon, cast on 57 sts.
Working in st st, cast off 6 sts at beg of next 2 rows.
Cont in st st, dec one st at beg of every row until 2 sts rem.
Cast off.

Bed-Roll

Using rust yarn, cast on 25 sts.
1st row. (P5, K5) twice, P5.
2nd row. (K5, P5) twice, K5.
Rep last 2 rows twice more.
7th row. (K5, P5) twice, K5.
8th row. (P5, K5) twice, P5.
Rep last 2 rows twice more.
Last 12 rows form patt.
Rep last 12 rows 4 times more, then work first 6 rows once more.
Cast off.

TO MAKE UP

Dye Head and Hands in tea (see **Note** page 38). Stitch Boot to Sole, having purl side of Sole facing outwards and cast-on edge of Sole forming toe end. Join back seam of Boot and centre top.

Join side seams, front and back seams and inside leg seams of Trousers.

Insert top of Boot into lower edge of Trousers and stitch in place. Join side edges of Top. Insert lower edge of Top into Trousers and stitch around waist edge. Fill with polyester filling through neck edge.

Stitch Belt and Buckle in position around waist, with purl side of Belt facing outwards.

Stitch navy yarn through top of Boots to form shoelaces.

Fold Hand pieces in half and stitch. Fold Sleeve (of Top) in half and join seam, leaving top and bottom edges open. Insert Hand into Sleeve and stitch in place.

Fill with polyester filling, stitch top opening closed.

Stitch Sleeves in position at shoulder edge of Top.

Join Head pieces, leaving neck edge open. Fill, then stitch to Top.

Take a single stitch through Head at each eye position, pull up slightly to define eyes, then tie ends in a knot.

Cut eyes from black felt and glue or stitch in position over knots.

Using navy wool, back-stitch above black felt eyes to create eyelids.

Using pink thread embroider nose, as photographed.

Using the maroon or rust yarn, embroider the mouth with a couple of stitches. Colour cheeks with lipstick, blusher or coloured pencil, if desired.

Hair and Beard. Using the method described for the Mammy doll's hair, on page 30, create coils of hair from brown wool. Stitch to doll's head and around his face, for a beard, trimming coil closely above the mouth to create a short moustache. Embroider his eyebrows with the same wool.

Hat. Stitch crown of Hat to brim. Mix 1 cup water with half a cup of PVA glue; mix well. Dip brim in PVA solution, squeeze out excess, leave to dry and stiffen. When dry, decorate Brim with corks.

Coat. Join shoulder seams. Join Sleeve seams. Sew in Sleeves, placing centre of Sleeves to shoulder seams. Join side seams. Sew buttons to Left Front. Fold top front edges of Fronts to right side of Fronts and stitch in place for lapels. Tie Scarf around neck.

Bed-Roll. Roll up Bed-Roll. Using 3mm hook and light brown yarn, crochet a length of ch long enough to go around each

end of rolled up Bed-Roll and over shoulder of Swagman.

Tie ends into a circle to fit around the rolled up Bed-Roll.

Billy. Cut away top one-third of the cardboard spice container. Paint it black and attach coathanger wire for handle.

Cockatoo. Using polymer clay, model a small white Cockatoo, as photographed, opposite, and harden according to the manufacturer's instructions.

-UPS

...he most discerning of dolls and teddies .... a complete knitted layette for baby, and all the bear essentials.

BEST DRESSED

From checked fabric, cut four Front/Backs, one 14cm x 33cm rectangle for bib, one 8cm x 9cm rectangle for pocket and two 8cm x 26cm strips for straps (all strip measurements *include* seam allowance).

Sewing

Fold bib in half crosswise, right sides together and stitch sides. Turn right side out, press and top-stitch about 5mm in from top and side edges. Neaten lower raw edges with zigzag stitch.

Press seam allowances to inside on lower and side edges of pocket, and finish upper raw edge with braid or ribbon. Top-stitch pocket onto centre of bib.

Join Front/Back side seams and inner leg seams. Place one leg inside the other, right sides together, and stitch crotch seam.

Press casing allowance to inside along fold line and turn under raw edge narrowly. Position bib on inside of trousers so that zigzagged edges of bib match folded lower edge of casing. Stitch casing in place, securing lower edge of bib at the same time. Top-stitch along upper edge of trousers, close to fold, making a second line of stitching across bib.

For *Cabbage Patch* doll, unpick side seams of casing and insert elastic to fit back waist. Secure ends.

Fold straps in half lengthwise, wrong sides together, press in raw edges and top-stitch close to all edges. Insert stud fasteners into top edges of bib and into ends of straps. Try overalls on for fit, adjust length of straps (they need to be much shorter for Cabbage Patch dolls), then hand-stitch straps in position on trousers back, angling the ends slightly so that straps can be crossed at back.

Press under raw edge narrowly on trouser legs and stitch. Turn under hem along fold line and slip-stitch in place. Turn hem to outside to form cuff.

OVERALLS

Measurements

To fit a 43cm teddy bear, or a Cabbage Patch doll if straps shortened and waist elasticised.

Materials

- 0.35m x 140cm checked fabric
- 0.10m x 3cm-wide braid or ribbon to bind pocket
- Two metal stud fasteners
- Small amount of 6mm elastic (Cabbage Patch doll)

Pattern piece

Pattern piece is printed on pattern sheet, Side 2, in black. Trace Front/Back 1A.

Cutting

Note. Remember to *add* 1.5cm seam allowance on Front/Back except on lower and upper edges where hem and casing allowances are already *included*.

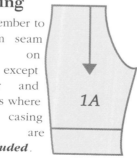

TEDDY'S BERET

Materials

- 20cm x 107cm fabric
- Co-ordinating wool for pom pom
- Thread

Cutting

From fabric cut one rectangle 59cm x 16cm for Top and one strip 43cm x 5cm for Band.

Sewing

Bring right sides of Top together along 16cm width and stitch. Run a gathering stitch along both 59cm edges. Pull one edge up very tightly to form top of beret and sew firmly to close top.

With right sides together pin and sew across 5cm width of Band and press seam open. Fold Band in half lengthways, wrong sides facing, and top-stitch three or four rows around band.

Ease gathers on remaining edge of top to fit band and, with right sides together, raw edges even, stitch top to band. Trim seam and neaten.

Make a small pom pom from wool and stitch to centre top.

TEDDY AND FRIEND

Every well-dressed bear, of course, goes out dressed in tartan overalls and matching beret, but at night he relaxes in a teddy-sized nightshirt and cosy nightcap. His little friend has a smart sailor dress and lacy underclothes, as well as a jumpsuit and night attire.

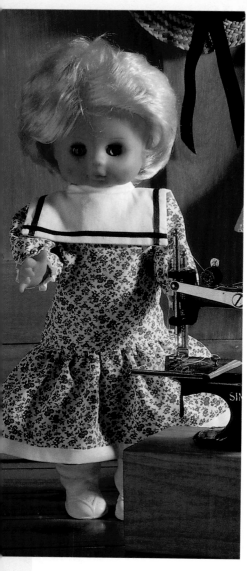

SAILOR DRESS

Measurements

To fit 42cm doll.

Materials

- 0.35m x 90cm cotton print
- 0.2m x 90cm white fabric
- 20cm elastic for wrists
- 65cm X 4mm-wide ribbon (optional)
- Two small press-studs
- Two small hooks

Pattern pieces

Pattern pieces are printed on the pattern sheet, Side 2, in black. Trace Front 5A, Back 6A, Front Collar 7A, Back Collar 8A and Sleeve 9A.

Cutting

Note. Remember to **add** 1cm seam allowance to all pieces.

From cotton print, cut one Front, two Backs, two Sleeves and one 11cm x 62cm rectangle for skirt (**includes** seam allowance).

From white fabric, cut two Front Collars, four Back Collars, one 4cm x 62cm strip for lower skirt binding, two 14cm x 4cm strips for Sleeve edges and one 17cm x 4cm bias strip for neck edge (all strip measurements **include** seam allowance).

Sewing

With right sides together, stitch centre back seam from lower edge to dot. Press seam allowance towards the left Back.

Narrowly finish raw edge of right-hand Back opening edge and press to wrong side on marked edge line, to form a 1cm-wide underlap for press-studs.

Turn under 1cm on lefthand Back opening edge and then press under again on marked edge line, to form overlap.

With right sides together, join Front to Backs at shoulder seams.

Make pleats in upper edges of Sleeves and baste in position.

With right sides facing, stitch Sleeves to armhole edges.

Fold strips for lower Sleeve edges in

half lengthwise, wrong sides together, and stitch on marked fold line to lower Sleeve edges, right sides together and raw edges even. Press turnings to wrong side and top-stitch 0.75cm in from lower Sleeve edges, forming a casing. Divide elastic and thread through Sleeve casings. Hand-stitch ends into place. With right sides together, stitch side and Sleeve seams in one continuous operation.

With right sides together, stitch each Front Collar to two Back Collars at shoulder seams. With right sides facing, stitch completed collar sections together around straight edges, leaving neck edge open. Turn collar right side out and press. Baste raw edges together.

If using ribbon, position it about 5mm in from finished edges of collar and top-stitch in place, carefully turning under raw ends.

With right sides facing and raw edges even, stitch collar to neck edge. Bind raw edges of neck with bias strip, slip-stitching inside edge of binding in place over neck seam and folding in raw edges at centre back.

Sew press-studs on centre back opening. Sew on hooks and work eyes on neck binding and lower edge of back collar.

With right sides facing, stitch short edges of skirt panel together. With right sides together, and raw edges even, stitch lower skirt binding to skirt panel. Fold under remaining raw edge of binding and slip-stitch over seam. Press.

Run a gathering thread around upper edge of skirt. Pull up gathers to fit and, with right sides facing, stitch skirt to bodice, matching centre back seams.

NIGHTSHIRT

Measurements

To fit 43cm teddy. Nightshirt will also fit Cabbage Patch doll.

Materials

- 0.7m x 140cm cotton print
- 0.9m x 4cm-wide bias binding
- Three buttons

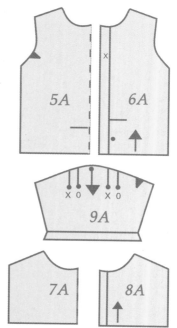

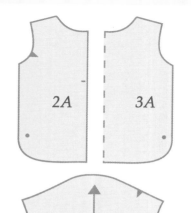

Pattern pieces

Pattern pieces are printed on the pattern sheet, Side 2, in black. Trace Front 2A, Back 3A and Sleeve 4A.

Cutting

Note. Remember to **add** 1cm seam allowances to all pieces and 6cm hem allowance to lower edges of Sleeves. The Sleeve pattern includes 4cm extra length for roll-back cuffs.

From cotton print, cut one Front, one Back, two Sleeves, two 10cm x 6cm strips for front bands (finished width 2cm) and one 34cm x 5cm strip for neckband (strip measurements **include** 1cm seam allowances).

Sewing

With right sides facing and raw edges even, stitch front bands to opening edges of Front, ensuring that both seams are made exactly the same

length and fastening seams on and off with a few back stitches. At corners, snip diagonally into seam allowances of Front (and not into band turnings). Fold overlap band lengthwise in half, right sides together, and stitch across narrow edges of lower end, exactly up to corner or join seam, respectively.

Fold underlap band in half, wrong sides together. Fold under long raw edge of underlap band and slipstitch to seam. Top-stitch close to finished edges. Baste lower edge of underlap band flat under horizontal edge of the opening and stitch seam allowance of Front carefully on to the underlap band.

Turn overlap band right side out. Fold under long raw edge of overlap and slipstitch to seam. Top-stitch long edge of overlap.

Baste overlap band flat on to underlap band and horizontal edge of opening, and stitch lower end into position. Top-stitch overlap band about 3cm up from this line of stitching, then stitch a diagonal cross between these two lines of stitching.

Bind lower edges of Front and Back with bias binding, up to dots on side seams.

With right sides together, stitch Front to Back at shoulders.

With right sides together, stitch Sleeves to armhole edges. Press seam allowances towards the shirt and top-stitch close to seams.

Press hem allowances of Sleeves to wrong side, fold under to half width and stitch in place.

With right sides together, sew side and Sleeve seams in one continuous operation, leaving side seams open below dots.

With right sides facing and raw edges even, stitch neck band to neck edge of nightshirt, remembering to extend band beyond front edges. Fold band in half, right sides together and stitch front edges even with bands. Trim excess from seam and turn band right side out. Fold under raw edge of inner band and slip-stitch to neck seam. Make two evenly spaced buttonholes in

front overlap band and one button-hole in neck band. Sew on buttons to correspond.

NIGHTCAP

Measurements

To fit a 43cm teddy bear.

Materials

- Approximately 40cm blue jersey
- Red wool or embroidery cotton

Sewing

Draw one quarter of a circle (35cm diameter) onto paper. The simplest way to do this is to pivot a 17.5cm length of thread around a fixed pin, marking the circle as you go.

Use the quarter circle as a pattern to cut out a piece of jersey.

Zigzag raw edges to neaten, then, with right sides together, join straight edges to form cap. Stitch under a 1cm hem on lower edge.

Make a tassel out of red wool or embroidery cotton and stitch to point of hat.

DOLL'S NIGHTDRESS

Measurements

To fit 42cm doll.

Materials

- 0.4m x 90cm fine white fabric
- 1.5m x 2.5cm-wide lace edging
- 1.1m x 0.75cm-wide satin ribbon
- Two small press-studs

Pattern pieces

All pattern pieces are printed on the pattern sheet, Side 2, in black.

Trace Front 14A, Back 15A and Sleeve 16A.

Cutting

Note. Remember to **add** 1cm seam allowance to all pieces.

From white fabric, cut one Front, two Backs and two Sleeves.

From lace edging, cut one 42cm length for neck edge, two 19cm lengths for wrists and one 63cm length for lower hem.

From ribbon, cut one 77cm length for neck (includes ties) and two approximately 10cm lengths for wrists (check doll's hand size first, as some have splayed fingers that won't go through narrow openings).

Sewing

With wrong sides together, stitch lace edging to Sleeves along seam line. Trim seam to 5mm and press towards upper Sleeve. Run a gathering thread along seam line of lower edge and draw up gathers to about 10cm width (or desired width for wrist, see Cutting instructions above). Stitch satin ribbon over trimmed seam allowance to secure gathers and hide seam

allowance. Repeat for other Sleeve.

With right sides together, stitch Sleeves to Front and Backs along raglan seamlines, matching symbols.

With right sides together, stitch Sleeve and side seams in one continuous operation.

Press seam allowances on centre back edges to inside.

Attach lace edging to neck edge, as for Sleeve edges. Run a gathering thread around neck edge and draw up gathers to about 17cm width. Stitch satin ribbon over seam, as for Sleeve edges, leaving 30cm of ribbon beyond neck edge on both sides, for ties.

With right sides together, stitch lace edging to lower edge of nightdress, then press the seam allowance upwards. Top-stitch close to seam to prevent rolling.

Finish raw edges of centre back opening and top-stitch along both edges. Tie ribbon at neck to close, and attach two small press-studs at intervals along opening.

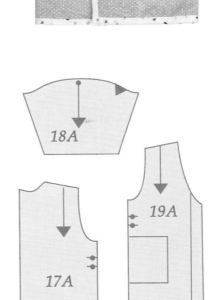

DRESSING GOWN

Measurements

To fit 42cm doll.

Materials

■ 0.4m x 90cm towelling
■ 2.4m x 3cm-wide bias binding (either purchased or self-made from cotton print)
■ Small amount of crochet cotton and hook (optional)

Pattern pieces

Pattern pieces are printed on the pattern sheet, Side 2, in black. Trace Front/Pocket 19A, Back 17A and Sleeve 18A.

Cutting

Note. Remember to **add** 1cm seam allowance to all pieces, except to the front opening edges, and lower edges

of both gown and Sleeves, as these edges will be bound.

From towelling, cut two Fronts, one Back, two Sleeves, two Pockets (allow seam allowance on one side only, where Pocket will be stitched into side seam; the other Pocket edges are bound) and one 3cm x 50cm strip for tie (strip measurements include seam allowance).

Sewing

Bind three edges of each Pocket piece with bias binding and top-stitch the binding close to seam edge. Position Pockets on Fronts, matching raw edges of side seams, and top-stitch in place close to one side and lower edges.

With right sides together, stitch Fronts to Back at shoulder seams.

With right sides together, and matching symbols, stitch Sleeves to

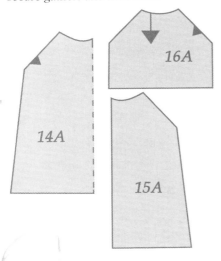

armhole edges. Bind lower edges of Sleeves with bias binding.

With right sides together, stitch Sleeve and side seams in one continuous operation, securing side edges of Pockets at the same time.

Beginning at one side seam, bind front, neck and lower edges of gown with bias binding.

Cut a piece of bias binding the same length as towelling strip for tie. With right sides facing, stitch the two pieces together, sewing diagonally across short ends to form points and leaving a small opening in one long side for turning. Turn and slip-stitch opening closed. Top-stitch around all edges.

With crochet cotton and hook, work a simple chain for belt loops and attach to dressing gown at small dots. You could also make these loops out of bias or towelling scraps, if desired.

JUMPSUIT

Measurements

To fit 42cm doll.

Materials

- 0.45cm x 90cm printed fabric
- Four small press-studs
- Four small buttons

Pattern pieces

Pattern pieces are printed on pattern sheet. Side 2, in black. Trace Bodice Front 10A, Trousers Front/Back 11A, Bodice Back 12A and Sleeve 13A.

Cutting

Note. Remember to **add** 1cm seam allowance to all pieces.

From printed fabric, cut two Bodice Fronts, four Trousers Front/Backs, one Bodice Back, two Sleeves and one 22cm x 4cm strip for neck binding (strip **includes** seam allowance).

Sewing

Fold lower edges of Sleeves and Trouser Front/Backs to wrong side

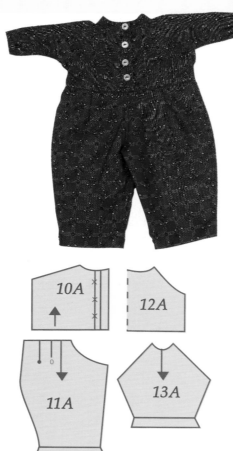

along given fold lines, turn under raw edges and hem in place by hand or machine.

With right sides together, stitch Sleeves to Front and Back Bodices along raglan seamlines. Press seam allowances towards bodice and top-stitch close to seams.

With right sides facing, stitch the Sleeve and bodice side seams in one continuous operation.

Narrowly finish raw edges of front opening and press to inside along given fold lines.

Bind neck edge with bias strip, slip-stitching inner edge of binding in place over neck seam and folding under raw edges at centre front.

Lap right front edge over left front edge, matching centre fronts and baste in position across lower edge.

Make pleats in upper edge of Trousers Front/Backs and baste.

With right sides together, join side seams and inner leg seams. Place one leg inside the other, right sides facing, and stitch crotch seam.

With right sides facing, stitch bodice to trousers, matching side seams and placing ends of crotch seam to centre front and back.

Attach top parts of press-studs under right front edge and the under parts onto the left front edge. Sew top press-stud onto neck binding. Sew buttons over press-studs on right front edge.

DOLL'S PANTIES

Measurements

To fit 42cm doll. Waist: 25.5cm.

Materials

- Scrap fine white fabric
- Approximately 0.45m x 1.5cm lace edging
- One small press-stud

Pattern pieces

Pattern pieces are printed on pattern sheet, Side 2, in black. Trace Front 20A and Back 21A.

Cutting

Note. Remember to **add** seam allowance to all pieces. From white fabric, cut two Fronts and two Backs.

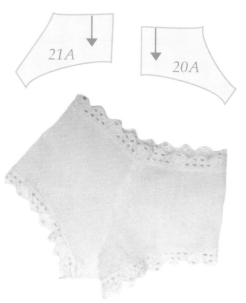

Sewing

With right sides together, stitch centre front seam of Fronts. Trim seam to 5mm and finish with a narrow zigzag stitch.

Stitch centre back seam of Backs as far as back opening. Trim seam below opening and finish as for Front. Above opening, press seam allowances to inside along seamline, fold under raw edges and stitch.

With right sides facing, stitch Front to Back at side seams.

Press under seam allowance around leg and waist edges. Place lace edging under folded edge so that it extends beyond fold, and top-stitch as close as possible to folded edge. On the inside, trim seam allowance very close to stitching. Then on the outside again, make a line of narrow zigzag stitch close to previous line of stitching which will finish raw edges.

At centre back, finish one end of lace flush with centre back fold line and allow the other a finished extension of about 1cm. On extended edge, sew the upper half of press-stud, and sew lower half to underlap to correspond.

With right sides together, stitch crotch seam. Trim to 5mm and zigzag. Press seam allowance towards front and top-stitch close to seam to keep it flat.

PETTICOAT

Measurements

To fit 42cm doll.

Materials

- ◼ 0.25m x 90cm fine white fabric
- ◼ 1.25m x 1.5cm lace edging
- ◼ Two small press-studs

Cutting

From white fabric, cut one 16.5cm x 10.5cm rectangle for bodice front, two 10.5cm squares for bodice backs and one 10.5cm x 61.5cm rectangle for skirt (all measurements **include** 1cm seam allowance).

Sewing

With right sides together, join bodice backs to bodice front at sides. Trim and neaten seams.

Press seam allowance to inside on one long (upper) edge of bodice. Cut a piece of lace edging the same length as upper edge (including seam allowances). Place lace along the inside of the upper edge so that edging extends beyond fold. Top-stitch lace in place very close to folded edge. On inside, trim seam allowance close to stitching line. Then, on outside again, zigzag along upper edge, which will neaten raw edges inside at the same time.

Trim 1cm from raw edge of left back opening only. Press under 0.5cm on raw edges of both back opening edges, then press under a further 1cm and stitch in place. Lap left back edge over right back edge about 1.5cm and baste across lower edge.

Cut a 61.5cm piece of lace edging and apply to one long (lower) edge of skirt, as for upper edge of bodice. With right sides together, stitch centre back seam of skirt.

Run a gathering thread around top edge of skirt and pull up gathers to fit bodice. With right sides together, and matching centre backs, stitch skirt to bodice. Trim and neaten seam.

Cut four pieces of lace edging, each 13.5cm long. Butt the raw edges of two pieces against one another and stitch with a close zigzag stitch, to form a strap. Repeat for other two pieces.

Pin straps onto inside upper edge of petticoat, then try garment on doll for fit. Adjust straps, angling as necessary to fit shoulders, hand-sew in place.

Sew on press-studs.

TEDDY'S ARGYLE JUMPER

Measurements

Fits chest: 40cm.
Actual measurement: 45cm.
Length: 18cm. Sleeve length: 9cm.

Materials

Panda Woolblend Crepe 8-ply (50g balls):
■ 2 balls Main Colour (MC, we used navy)
■ I ball each 1st Contrast (C1, we used red), 2nd Contrast (C2, we used green), and 3rd Contrast (C3, we used yellow) for knitting-stitch embroidery
■ One pair each 3.25mm (No 10) and 4mm (No 8) knitting needles
■ Two stitch-holders
■ Knitter's needle for sewing seams and embroidery
■ Two buttons

Tension: See Knitting and Crochet Notes on page 120.
22sts and 30 rows to 10cm over st st, using 4mm needles.

Back

Using MC and 3.25mm needles, cast on 46 sts.

1st row. K2,*P2; rep from * to end.
2nd row. P2,*K2, P2; rep from * to end.
Rep 1st and 2nd rows until work measures 2cm, ending with a 2nd row and inc 5 sts evenly across last row...51 sts.
Change to 4mm needles.
Cont in st st until work measures 7cm from beg, ending with a purl row.
Note. When changing colours in the middle of a row, twist the colour to be used underneath and to the right of colour just used, making sure both yarns are worked firmly at joins. Always change colours on wrong side of work so colour change does not show on right side. Use a separate ball of yarn for each section of colour; wind yarn into smaller balls if necessary.
Work rows 1 to 15 incl from Graph below, tying a marker at each end of 1st row to mark beg of armholes, as there is no armhole shaping, and noting to work C3 in knitting-stitch embroidery when making up.
Cont in MC st st until work measures 17cm from beg, beg and ending with a purl row.
Shape shoulders. Cast off 4 sts at beg of next 8 rows.
Leave rem 19 sts on a stitch-holder.

Front

Work as for Back until there are 6 rows less than Back to beg of shoulder shaping, thus ending with a purl row.
Shape neck. Next row. K20, *turn.*
Cont on these 20 sts, dec one st at neck edge in next row...19 sts.
Note. This side of neck is 4 rows lower to accommodate Shoulder Band.
Shape shoulder. Cast off 4 sts at beg of next and foll alt rows 3 times in all, AT THE SAME TIME dec one st at neck edge in every row 3 times.
Work one row. Cast off rem 4 sts.
With right side facing, sl next 11 sts on a stitch-holder.
Join MC to rem 20 sts and knit to end.
Cont on these 20 sts, dec one st at neck edge in next 4 rows...16 sts.
Work 2 rows.
Shape shoulder. Complete as for other shoulder, omitting dec at neck edge.

Sleeves

Using MC and 3.25mm needles, cast on 38 sts.
Work in rib as for Back for 2cm, ending with a 2nd row and inc 3 sts evenly across last row...41 sts.
Change to 4mm needles.
Cont in st st, inc one st at each end of 5th and foll alt rows until there are 49 sts, then in foll 4th row once...51 sts.
Cont straight in st st until work measures 9cm from beg, beg and ending with a purl row.
Shape top. Cast off 5 sts at beg of next 8 rows. Cast off rem 11 sts.

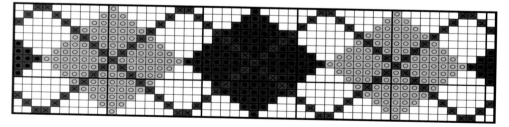

When working from graph, read odd-numbered rows (knit rows) from right to left, and even numbered rows (purl rows) from left to right. Work C3 knitting-stitch embroidery when making up garment. 1sq = 1st.

□ = MC   ▨ = C1   ◉ = C2   ■ = C3

Neckband

Join right shoulder seam. With right side facing, using MC and 3.25mm needles, knit up 44 sts evenly along neck edge, incl sts from stitch holders.

1st row. P3, *K2, P2; rep from * to last st, P1.

2nd row. K3, *P2, K2; rep from * to last st. K1. Rep 1st and 2nd rows once, then 1st row once (5 rows rib).

Cast off loosely in rib.

Left Front
Shoulder Band

With right side facing, using MC and 3.25mm needles, knit up 23 sts evenly along left front shoulder and end of Neckband.

1st row. P2, *K2, P2; rep from * to last st, P1.

2nd row. Rib 7, yon, rib 2tog, rib 8, yon, rib 2tog, rib 4...2 buttonholes.

Rep 1st and 2nd rows once, then 1st row once.

Cast off loosely in rib.

Left Back
Shoulder Band

Work as for Left Front Shoulder Band, omitting buttonholes.

To make up

Overlap Front Shoulder Band over Back Shoulder Band and oversew at armhole edge.

Using knitting-stitch and C3, work embroidery from Graph, page 52, on Back and Front of Jumper.

Sew in Sleeves evenly between markers, placing centre of Sleeves to shoulder seams. Join side and Sleeve seams.

Sew on buttons.

TEDDY'S CARDIGAN

Materials

Panda Woolblend Crepe 8-ply:
- 2 balls
- One pair each 3.25mm (No 10) and 4mm (No 8) knitting needles

Measurements

Fits chest: 40cm. Actual measurement: 45cm. Length: 18cm. Sleeve length: 9cm.

- One stitch-holder
- One cable needle
- Knitter's needle for sewing seams
- Three buttons

Tension: See Knitting and Crochet Notes on page 120.

22 sts and 30 rows to 10cm over st st, using 4mm needles.

Special abbreviations: C4B: sl next 2 sts on cable needle and leave at back of work, K2, then K2 from cable needle.

C4F: sl next 2 sts on cable needle and leave at front of work, K2, then K2 from cable needle.

Back

Using 3.25mm needles, cast on 54 sts.

1st row. K2, *P2, K2; rep from * to end.

2nd row. P2, *K2, P2; rep from * to end. Rep 1st and 2nd rows until work measures 2cm from beg, ending with a 2nd row and inc 4 sts evenly across last row...58 sts.

Change to 4mm needles and beg patt.

1st row. (K2, P2) twice, K2, P1, K8, P1, (K2, P2) 4 times, K2, P1, K8, P1, (K2, P2) twice, K2.

2nd row. (P2, K2) twice, P2, K1, P8, K1, (P2, K2) 4 times, P2, K1, P8, K1, (P2, K2) twice, P2.

3rd row. (P2, K2) twice, P3, C4B, C4F, P3, (K2, P2) 4 times, P1, C4B, C4F, P3, (K2, P2) twice.

4th row. (K2, P2) twice, K3, P8, K3, (P2, K2) 4 times, K1, P8, K3, (P2, K2) twice.

Rows 1 to 4 incl form patt.

Cont in patt until work measures 9cm from beg, ending with a wrong-side row. Work 26 rows patt.

Shape shoulders. Keeping patt correct, cast off 10 sts at beg of next 4 rows.

Leave rem 18 sts on stitch-holder.

Left Front

Using 3.25mm needles, cast on 27 sts.

1st row. K2, *P2, K2; rep from * to last st, K1.

2nd row. P3, *K2, P2; rep from * to end. Rep 1st and 2nd rows until work measures 2cm, ending with a 2nd row and inc one st in centre of last row...28 sts. Change to 4mm needles.

1st row. (K2, P2) twice, K2, P1, K8, P1, (K2, P2) twice.

2nd row. (K2, P2) twice, K1, P8, K1, (P2, K2) twice, P2.

3rd row. (P2, K2) twice, P3, C4B, C4F, P3, K2, P2, K2.

4th row. (P2, K2) twice, K1, P8, K3, (P2, K2) twice.

Rows 1 to 4 incl form patt.

Cont in patt until work measures 9cm from beg, ending with a wrong-side row.

Shape front slope. Keeping patt correct, dec one st at end (front edge) of next and foll alt rows 3 times in all, then in foll 4th rows until 20 sts rem. Work one row.

Shape shoulder. Keeping patt correct, cast off 10 sts at beg of next row. Work one row.

Cast off rem 10sts.

Right Front

Using 3.25 needles, cast on 27 sts.

1st row. K2, *P2, K2; rep from * to last st, K1.

2nd row. P3, *K2, P2; rep from * to end.

Rep 1st and 2nd rows until work measures 2cm from beg, ending with a 2nd row and inc one st in centre of last row...28sts.

Change to 4mm needles.

1st row. (P2. K2) twice, P1, K8, P1, (K2. P2) twice, K2.

2nd row. (P2, K2) twice, P2, K1, P8, K1, (P2, K2) twice.

3rd row. (K2, P2) twice, P1, C4B, C4F, P3, (K2, P2) twice.

4th row. (K2, P2) twice, K3, P8, K3, P2, K2, P2.

Rows 1 to 4 incl form patt.

Complete as for Left Front, reversing all shapings.

Sleeves

Using 3.25mm needles, cast on 34 sts. Work in rib as given for Back for 2cm, ending with a 2nd row and inc 8 sts evenly across last row...42 sts.

Change to 4mm needles.

1st row. (P2, K2) 4 times, P1, K8, P1, (K2, P2) 4 times.

2nd row. (K2, P2) 4 times, K1, P8, K1, (P2, K2) 4 times.

3rd row. (K2, P2) 4 times, P1, C4B, C4F, P1, (P2, K2) 4 times.

4th row. (P2, K2) 4 times, K1, P8, K1, (K2, P2) 4 times.

Cont in patt as placed in last 4 rows, inc one st at each end of next and foll 4th rows until there are 50 sts, working all extra sts in side edge patt.

Cont straight in patt until work measures 9cm from beg, ending with a wrong-side row.

Shape top. Keeping patt correct, cast off 9 sts at beg of next 4 rows.

Cast off rem 14 sts.

Left Front Band

Join shoulder seams.

With right side facing and using 3.25mm needles, beg at centre Back neck and knit across 9 sts from half of the Back stitch-holder, knit up 27 sts evenly along Front slope shaping, then knit up 26 sts evenly along Front edge...62 sts.

Work one row rib as for 2nd row of Back.

Next row. Rib to last 26 sts, yfwd, rib 2tog, (rib 9, yfwd, rib 2tog) twice, rib 2...3 buttonholes.

Work 3 rows rib.

Cast off loosely in rib.

Right Front Band

Work as for Left Front Band, beginning at the lower edge and omitting the buttonholes.

To make up

Tie a marker 11cm down from the beginning of the shoulder shaping on side edges of Back and Fronts to mark the armholes.

Sew in the Sleeves evenly between the markers, placing centre of Sleeves to shoulder seams. Join side and Sleeve seams. Join the Bands at centre Back. Sew on buttons.

BABY DOLL'S LAYETTE

Measurements

Layette fits a 40cm Baby Doll with a 26cm chest. Dress measures 28cm; length: 24cm; Sleeve: 3cm. Jacket measures 30cm; length: 16cm; Sleeve: 7cm. The Bonnet measures 26cm around face. Bootees fit 6.5cm foot.

Materials

Patons Patonyle 4-ply (50g):
- 2 balls
- One pair 3.25mm (No 10) knitting needles
- Three stitch-holders
- Two buttons for Dress
- Three buttons for Jacket
- Embroidery threads for Dress and Jacket
- Embroidery needle
- Ribbon for Bonnet and Bootees

Tension

See Knitting and Crochet Notes on page 120.
29 sts and 38.5 rows to 10cm over st st, using 3.25mm needles.

DRESS

Back

Cast on 83 sts.
1st row. K1, *P1, K1; rep from * to end.
Rep last row 7 times more for moss st. Work 4 rows st st, then 6 rows moss st.
Cont in st st until work measures 16cm from beg, ending with a knit row.
Next row. P1, *p2tog; rep from * to last 2 sts, P2...43 sts.
Work 6 rows moss st.
Shape armholes. Working rem in st st, cast off 3 sts at beg of next 2 rows, then dec one st at each end of next

and foll alt rows until 31 sts rem. **
Work one row.
Divide for back opening.
1st row. K14, (Pl, Kl) twice, turn and cont on these 18 sts.
2nd row. (K1, P1) twice, K1, purl to end.
3rd row. Knit to last 4 sts, (P1, K1) twice.
Rep 2nd and 3rd rows twice, then 2nd row once.
9th row. Knit to last 4 sts, P1, yrn, P2tog (buttonhole), K1.
Rep 2nd and 3rd rows twice, then 2nd row once.
Shape shoulder. Keeping border correct, cast off 7 sts at beg of next row.
Work one row.
Leave rem 11 sts on a stitch-holder.
With right side facing, join yarn to rem 13 sts, cast on 5 sts for underlap, work (Kl, P1) twice over first 4 sts of these 18 sts, knit to end.
2nd row. Purl to last 5 sts, (Kl, P1) twice, K1.
3rd row. (K1, P1) twice, knit to end.
Rep last 2 rows 6 times.
Shape shoulder. Keeping border correct, cast off 7 sts at beg of next row.
Leave rem 11 sts on a stitch-holder.

Front

Work as for Back to **.
Work a further 3 rows st st.
Shape neck. Next row. K12, *turn*.
Cont in st st on these 12 sts, dec one st at neck edge in alt rows until 7 sts rem.
Work 9 rows.
Cast off.
With right side facing, sl next 7 sts on a stitch-holder and leave.
Join yarn to rem 12 sts and work to correspond with side just completed, reversing shaping.

Sleeves

Cast on 31 sts.
Work 6 rows moss st, inc 4 sts evenly across last row...35 sts.
Work 6 rows st st.
Shape top. Cont in st st, cast off 2 sts at beg of next 2 rows, then dec one st at each end of every row until 11 sts rem. Cast off loosely.

Neckband

Using a flat seam, join shoulder seams. With right side facing, patt across sts from Left Back stitch-holder; knit up 39 sts evenly around Front neck (incl sts from stitch-holder), then patt across sts from Right Back stitch-holder...61 sts.
Work 5 rows moss st, working a buttonhole (as before) in 2nd row.
Cast off in moss st.

To make up

Do not press. Using backstitch, join side and Sleeve seams. Sew in Sleeves, placing centre of Sleeves 4 rows to front of shoulder seam.
Sew underlap in position. Sew on the buttons. Embroider three bullion-stitch roses at centre front of yoke.

JACKET
(worked in one piece to armholes)

Cast on l35 sts.
Work 6 rows moss st.
7th row. (Kl, P1) twice, knit to last 4 sts, (P1, Kl) twice.
8th row. (Kl, P1) twice, Kl, purl to last 5 sts, (Kl, P1) twice, K1.
Rep 7th and 8th rows until work measures 8cm from beg, ending with a 7th row.
Next row. Moss st 5 sts, P2tog, *P1, P2tog; rep from * to last 5 sts, moss st 5 sts...93 sts.
Work 2 rows moss st.

Next row. K1, P1, yrn, P2tog (button-hole), moss st to end.

Work 3 rows moss st.

Divide for armholes. Next row.
(K1, P1) twice, K18, cast off 5 sts, K39, cast off 5 sts, K18, (P1, KI) twice.

Cont on last 22 sts for Left Front.

Keeping 5 sts in moss st at front edge and working rem sts in st st, dec one st at armhole edge in alt rows until 18 sts rem.

Work 5 rows.

Shape neck. Next row. Knit to last 7 sts, turn, leave these 7 sts on a stitch-holder.

Cont in st st on rem 11 sts, dec one st at neck edge in alt rows until 7 sts rem.

Work 9 rows.

Cast off.

With wrong side facing, join yarn to next 39 sts for Back.

Working in st st, dec one st at each end of alt rows until 31 sts rem.

Work 15 rows st st.

Shape shoulders. Cont in st st, cast off 7 sts at beg of next 2 rows.

Leave rem 17 sts on a stitchholder.

With wrong side facing, join yarn to rem 22 sts for Right Front.

Keeping 5 sts in moss st at front edge and working rem sts in st st, dec one st at armhole edge in alt rows until 18 sts rem, at the same time, working a buttonhole (as before) in 10th row from previous buttonhole.

Work 6 rows.

Shape neck. Next row. Purl to last 7 sts, turn, leave these 7 sts on a stitch-holder.

Complete to correspond with Left Front.

Sleeves

Cast on 31 sts.

Work 6 rows moss st, inc 4 sts evenly across last row...35 sts.

Cont in st st, inc one st at each end of 7th row and foll 6th row...39 sts.

Cont straight in st st until work measures 7cm from beg, ending with a purl row.

Shape top. Cont in st st, cast off 2 sts at beg of next 2 rows, then dec one st at each end of every row until 11 sts rem.

Cast off loosely.

Neckband

Using a flat seam, join shoulder seams. With right side facing, sl sts from Right Front stitch-holder on to needle, then use same needle to knit up 43 sts evenly around neck (incl sts from Back stitch-holder), then patt across sts from Left Front stitch-holder...57 sts.

Work 5 rows moss st, working a buttonhole (as before) in 2nd row.

Cast off in moss st.

To make up

Do not press. Using backstitch, join Sleeve seams, then sew in Sleeves, placing centre of Sleeve 4 rows to front of shoulder seam. Sew on buttons. Embroider a bullion-stitch rose on each Front yoke.

BONNET

Cast on 73 sts.

Work 6 rows moss st.

7th row. (K1, P1) twice, knit to last 4 sts, (P1, K1) twice.

8th row. (K1, P1) twice, K1, purl to last 5 sts, (K1, P1) twice, K1.

Rep 7th and 8th rows until the work

measures 7cm from beg, ending with an 8th row.

Shape back. 1st row. K1, *K2tog, K7; rep from * to end...65sts.

2nd and 4th rows. K1, purl to last st, K1.

3rd row. K1, *K2tog, K6; rep from * to end...57 sts.

5th row. K1, *K2tog, K5; rep from * to end...49 sts.

Cont dec in this manner (working one st less between decs each time) in alt rows until 17 sts rem. Break off yarn, run end through rem sts, draw up tightly and fasten off securely.

To make up

Do not press. Using a flat seam, join back seam. Sew ribbon in position.

BOOTEES
(beg at sole)

Cast on 31 sts.

1st row. *Inc in next st, K13, inc in next st; rep from * once, K1...35sts.

2nd and alt rows. K1, purl to last st, K1.

3rd row. *Inc in next st, K15, inc in next st; rep from * once, K1...39sts.

5th row. *Inc in next st, K17, inc in next st; rep from * once, K1...43sts.

7th row. *Inc in next st, K19, inc in next st; rep from * once, K1...47sts.

9th row. Knit.

10th row. As 2nd row.

Shape instep. 1st row. K27, sl 1, K1, psso, *turn.*

2nd row. P8, P2tog, *turn.*

3rd row. K8, sl 1, K1, psso, *turn.*
Rep 2nd and 3rd rows 6 times, then 2nd row once.

17th row. Knit to end...31 sts.

18th row. K1, purl to last st, K1.

19th row (eyelets). K1, *K1, yfwd, K2tog; rep from * to end.

20th row. As 18th row.

Work 10 rows moss st.

Cast off in moss st.

To make up

Do not press. Using a flat seam, join leg and foot seams. Thread ribbon through eyelet holes at ankle.

PERIOD
FINERY

Take your pick from a Regency
belle, an Edwardian miss or a
young lady from the '50s, each
outfit complete with
accessories such as a full set of
underwear, shoes and hat.

COSTUME FINERY FOR DOLLS

Measurements

Regency, Edwardian and Modern costumes are made from one basic pattern to fit doll 40cm tall.

REGENCY DOLL

Materials

■ 0.45m x 90cm fine white fabric, such as lawn or batiste, for pantaloons and petticoat
■ Opaque white pantihose or baby tights, for stockings
■ 0.5m x 115cm striped fabric (sprigged floral is also suitable), for dress and bonnet
■ 0.15m x 90cm fine cream fabric, such as lawn or batiste
■ 0.15m x 90cm iron-on interfacing
■ Four tiny press-studs
■ 1.3m x 2.5cm-wide cotton lace edging, for underwear
■ 0.4m x 1.5cm-wide cotton beading, for pantaloons
■ 1.5m x 2cm-wide cream lace edging, for dress
■ 0.7m x 3.5cm-wide cream cotton lace, for bonnet
■ 1m x 1cm-wide satin ribbon, for bonnet
■ 0.65m x 5mm-wide white satin ribbon
■ 0.5m x 2mm-wide satin ribbon, for Reticule
■ Eight tiny purchased ribbon roses, for bonnet and shoes
■ Strong craft glue
■ Small amount stuffing, for Reticule

Pattern pieces

All pattern pieces, except rectangles, are printed on the pattern sheet, Side 4, in black. Trace Pantaloons Front, Pantaloons Back, Dress/Petticoat Bodice Front, Modesty Panel, Dress/Petticoat Bodice Back, Sleeve, Hat Brim, Hat Crown, Hat Back Crown, Stocking and Reticule.

Cutting

Note. A 6mm seam allowance is included on all pieces unless otherwise specified.

From white fabric, cut two Pantaloon Fronts, two Pantaloon Backs, two Petticoat Bodice Fronts (cutting to Edwardian neckline, but Regency bodice line), two Petticoat Bodice Backs (cutting to Regency bodice line), and one rectangle, 75cm x 20cm, for Skirt.

From opaque tights, cut two Stockings.

From striped fabric, cut one Dress Bodice Front (cutting to Regency neckline and bodice line), two Dress Bodice Backs (cutting to Regency bodice line), two Sleeves (cutting to

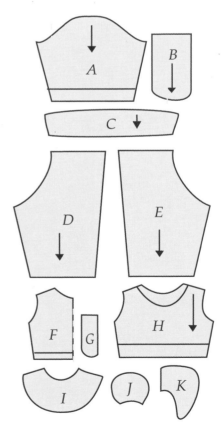

A: Sleeve. B: Reticule. C: Hat crown. D: Pantaloons front. E: Pantaloons back. F: Dress /petticoat/Blouse bodice back. G: Stocking. H: Dress/ petticoat/Blouse bodice front. I: Regency modesty panel. J: Hat crown back. K: Hat brim.

Regency line), two rectangles, each 9cm x 5cm, for Lower Sleeves, one rectangle, 75cm x 23cm for Skirt, one Hat Brim, two Hat Crowns, two Hat Back Crowns and one Reticule.

Cut also a strip of striped fabric, 2.5cm x 30cm, for a Waistband and another, 2.5cm x 24cm, to trim bonnet (optional).

From cream fabric, cut one Dress Bodice Front for bodice lining (cutting to Edwardian neckline, but Regency bodice line). Remainder of cream fabric will be cut after it has been pintucked (see instructions below).

From interfacing, cut one Hat Brim, one Hat Crown and one Hat Back Crown.

Sewing

PANTALOONS

Stitch Pantaloon Fronts and Backs together at side and inside leg seams – we used narrow French seams for added neatness. With right sides together, stitch crotch seam from front to back; neaten seam with fine zigzag.

Press 6mm to outside along top edge. Position lace beading on outside along top edge and stitch in place close to both edges, concealing raw edge and folding in raw edges of beading. Thread white satin ribbon through beading, starting and finishing at centre front and draw up to fit waist. Make a narrow rolled hem on lower edges of pantaloons and whip-stitch cotton lace edging in place, neatening raw edges of lace at inside leg seam.

PETTICOAT

With right sides together, stitch Petticoat Bodice Fronts to Bodice Backs at shoulders, forming a single piece, which becomes both bodice and bodice lining (see Diagram, page 64). Press seams open. With right sides together, stitch armhole and neck edges, trim seams and clip curves. Turn right side out and press. Open out sides so that underarm seams and

lower edges match on each side and, with right sides together, stitch through in one long seam.

Turn right side out by pulling backs through shoulders and press again.

With right sides together, stitch centre back seam of Skirt, allowing a 1.5cm seam and stopping stitching 10cm below upper edge, to allow for back opening. Neaten raw edges of seam allowance, then press seam to one side, including unstitched section.

Run a gathering thread along upper edge of Skirt and draw up gathers to fit bodice. With right sides facing, pin Skirt to bodice, adjust gathers and stitch, taking care not to catch bodice lining in seam. Press under raw edge of bodice lining and slip-stitch pressed edge in place over seam. Lap Bodice Backs and stitch press-studs in place.

Press under raw edge on lower edge of Skirt and stitch cotton lace edging in place to conceal raw edge, neatening raw ends of lace at centre back.

STOCKINGS

Fold Stockings in half lengthwise along fold line, right sides together, and stitch seam close to edge using narrow zigzag or stretch stitch. Turn right side out.

DRESS

Make narrow and even pintucks across remaining cream fabric to give sufficient pintucked fabric to cut one Modesty Panel and one Hat Brim. Cut these pieces, taking care to position pintucking exactly along straight grain.

Stitch around seam line on neck edge of Bodice Front then snip through seam allowance as far as stitching and press under seam allowance. Place pintucked Modesty Panel behind pressed neckline of Bodice Front and topstitch Bodice to Panel, stitching as close to pressed neckline as possible.

With right sides together, stitch Bodice Fronts to Bodice Backs at shoulders, as for Petticoat (see Diagram, page 64). Press seams open.

Cut a piece of cream lace edging twice length of neck edge plus turning allowance (approximately 40cm). Run a gathering thread along straight edge of lace and pull up to fit neck edge, turning under raw edges at either end. With right sides facing and raw edges even, baste gathered lace to neck edge of bodice. With right sides together, stitch bodice to bodice lining around

neck edge, sandwiching lace at the same time. Clip curves, turn right side out and press. Baste raw edges together at armhole, sides and lower edges.

Run a gathering thread along upper and lower edges of Sleeves. Draw up gathers on lower edge to fit 9cm edge of Lower Sleeve and, with right sides together, stitch Sleeve to Lower Sleeve. Trim and neaten seam. Repeat for remaining Sleeve.

With right sides together, pin Sleeves to bodice and draw up gathers to fit. Stitch Sleeve to armhole, trim and neaten seam.

Cut two pieces of cream lace edging, each twice the length of sleeve edge, plus turning allowance (approximately 20-25cm each). Run a gathering thread along straight edge of lace, pull up gathers to fit sleeve edge and stitch gathered lace in place by hand or machine.

With right sides facing, stitch bodice fronts to backs at sides and underarms, continuing through cuffs and lace trim in one seam. Trim and neaten seam.

With right sides together, stitch centre back seam of Skirt, allowing a 1.5cm seam and stopping stitching 10cm below top edge to allow for opening. Finish back opening as for Petticoat, above. Ascertain centre front of Skirt and mark with a pin.

Beginning approximately 4cm from centre front on both sides, run a gathering thread around top edge of Skirt.

With right sides together, pin Skirt to bodice, matching centre fronts. Draw up gathers to fit, noting that 8cm at centre front is ungathered, baste and stitch. Trim seam and neaten.

Turn up a narrow hem on lower edge of Skirt and finish by machine or hand. Cut cream lace edging to fit lower edge and handstitch in place, neatening lace ends at centre back.

Press under long raw edges of Waistband strip and slip-stitch neatly in

place on bodice to conceal seam between bodice and Skirt, turning under raw edges at centre back.

Lap Bodice Backs and sew on press-studs to close.

BONNET

Press interfacing to wrong side of one Bonnet Brim (not the pintucked piece), one Crown and one Back Crown. Remaining pieces form bonnet lining.

With right sides together, stitch Brim to Crown, then Crown to Back Crown, easing where necessary. Repeat for bonnet lining. Clip curves and neaten seams. With right sides facing, stitch bonnet to bonnet lining around outer edge of Brim. Neaten and clip seam, turn right side out and press.

Push bonnet lining into bonnet, wrong sides together, turn in neck edges of bonnet and lining and slip-stitch opening closed.

Run a gathering thread along straight edge of 3.5cm-wide cotton lace edging and draw up to fit around inside brim and neck edge of bonnet, allowing overlap at centre back. Adjust gathers to fit and slip-stitch lace neatly in place around inner brim seam and neck edge of bonnet. Press under raw edges on bonnet band, if using, and slip-stitch to front of Crown, behind Brim.

Cut satin ribbon in half and stitch to either side of Crown on band, for ties. Glue three tiny ribbon roses to each side of bonnet over tie ends, to decorate.

RETICULE

Fold Reticule in half, right sides together, and stitch around outer edge, leaving top unstitched. Fold in top edge. Fill with a tiny amount of stuffing or scrap fabric, then tie 2mm ribbon tightly about 5cm from top edge, leaving large loops in bow for handles.

SHOES

Glue a small ribbon rose to centre front of purchased shoes.

EDWARDIAN DOLL'S CLOTHES

Materials

■ 0.45m x 90cm fine white fabric, such as lawn or batiste, for pantaloons and petticoat
■ Opaque white pantihose or baby tights, for stockings
■ 0.3m x 115cm velvet, for dress
■ 0.15m x 90cm lining fabric, for bodice
■ 0.4m x 115cm white cotton fabric, for pinafore
■ 1.3m x 2.5cm-wide cotton lace edging, for underwear
■ 0.4m x 1.5cm-wide cotton beading, for pantaloons
■ 0.65m x 5mm-wide white satin ribbon
■ 0.45m x 3.5cm-wide white satin ribbon
■ 0.7m x 15cm-wide white lace edging
■ 1m x 2.5cm-wide grosgrain ribbon
■ 0.7m x 2cm-wide broderie anglaise beading
■ 0.7m x 4cm-wide broderie anglaise edging
■ 1m x 0.5cm-wide burgundy velvet ribbon
■ Six tiny press-studs
■ Two small pearl buttons
■ Six purchased ribbon roses, for dress and hat
■ Ready-made straw hat
■ 30cm x 1.5cm-wide grosgrain ribbon
■ Scraps of fine black leather, vinyl or felt, for shoes
■ Black paint or shoe dye
■ Six tiny pearl beads, for shoe buttons

Pattern pieces

All pattern pieces, except rectangles, are printed in on pattern sheet, Side 4, in black. Trace Pantaloons Front, Pantaloons Back, Dress/Petticoat Bodice Front, Dress/Petticoat Bodice Back, Sleeve, Pinafore Bodice Front, Pinafore Bodice Back, Stocking and Shoe Upper.

Cutting

Note. 6mm seam allowance is included on all pieces, except Shoe Upper unless otherwise specified.

From white fabric, cut two Pantaloon Fronts, two Pantaloon Backs, two Petticoat Bodice Fronts (cutting to Edwardian neckline and bodice line), two Petticoat Bodice Backs (cutting to Edwardian bodice line), and one rectangle, 75cm x 14cm, for Skirt.

From opaque tights, cut two Stockings.

From velvet, cut one Bodice Front (cutting to Edwardian bodice line), two Bodice Backs (note: do not cut Bodice Backs on fold; add seam allowance to fold line and cut two single pieces, to Edwardian bodice line), two Sleeves, one 3cm x 11cm rectangle for Collar and one 75cm x 20cm rectangle for Skirt.

From lining, cut one Bodice Front and two Bodice Backs, with added seam allowance at centre back, as above.

From white cotton fabric, cut two Pinafore Bodice Fronts, two Pinafore Bodice Backs, one rectangle, 15cm x 70cm, for Skirt, and one rectangle, 10cm x 110cm, for Frill.

From leather, vinyl or felt, cut two Shoe Uppers.

Sewing

PANTALOONS PETTICOAT AND STOCKINGS

Make as for Regency Pantaloons, Petticoat and Stockings, on page 61, but use three press-studs on back opening of Petticoat instead of two.

DRESS

Press and baste 0.5cm tucks across 3.5cm-wide satin ribbon at 1cm intervals, to give the effect of pin-tucking or ruching. Make a piece approximately 14cm long and stitch to centre front of Bodice Front.

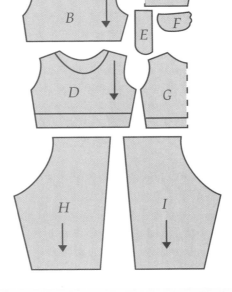

Apply a strip of white lace edging to either side of ribbon tucking, to conceal edges of ribbon.

With right sides together, stitch Bodice Front to Bodice Backs at shoulder seams and press seams open. Repeat for bodice lining. With right sides together, stitch bodice to bodice lining at centre back seams. Turn lining to inside, press and baste raw neck, armhole and side seams together.

With right sides together and raw edges even, stitch Collar to neck edge. Press under remaining raw edge on Collar and slip-stitch pressed edge over neck seam, turning in ends neatly at back opening edges.

Finish lower edge of Sleeves with white lace, gathering Sleeve onto lace as necessary to fit over doll's wrist.

Run a gathering thread around crown of Sleeve. With right sides together, pin Sleeve to bodice, draw up gathers to fit and stitch. Trim and neaten seam.

With right sides facing, stitch bodice fronts to backs at sides and underarms, continuing through lace trim in one seam. Trim and neaten seam.

With right sides together, stitch centre back seam of Skirt, allowing a 1.5cm seam and leaving 8cm unstitched from top, for back opening. Neaten raw edges of seam allowance, then press seam to one side, including unstitched section. Beginning 4cm from lower edge of Skirt, stitch five pintucks, 1cm apart around Skirt. Run a gathering thread around top edge of Skirt. With right sides facing, pin Skirt to bodice, pull up gathers to fit and stitch. Try garment on doll and pin hem so that lace on petticoat shows beneath dress skirt. Hem skirt by hand.

A: Sleeve. B: Pinafore/bodice front.
C: Pinafore/bodice back.
D: Dress/ petticoat/Blouse bodice front. E: Stocking. F: Shoe upper.
G: Dress/ petticoat/Blouse bodice back. H: Pantaloons front.
I: Pantaloons back.

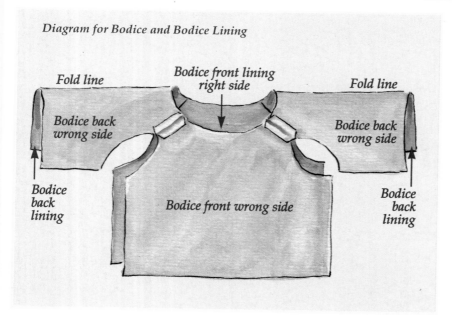

Diagram for Bodice and Bodice Lining

Fold line

Bodice front lining right side

Fold line

Bodice back wrong side

Bodice back wrong side

Bodice back lining

Bodice front wrong side

Bodice back lining

Ascertain centre point of grosgrain ribbon and position this point at centre front of bodice, with lower edge of ribbon just concealing waistline. Stitch along both edges of ribbon beginning and ending 4cm in from back opening to allow for neat tying of bow at centre back.

Stitch or glue roses to neckline at centre front. Lap Bodice Backs and stitch three press-studs in position to close.

PINAFORE

Make up Pinafore bodice as for Petticoat, on page 61, but before stitching armhole edges, cut two pieces of broderie anglaise edging, each twice the length of armhole plus turning allowance. Run a gathering thread along straight edge of each and, with right sides together and raw edges even, pin broderie anglaise to armhole edge of pinafore bodice. Draw up gathers to fit and baste. When armhole seam is stitched, broderie anglaise will be sandwiched at the same time. Neaten raw edges at underarm.

Make a narrow machine-stitched hem on each short end of Skirt, then run a gathering thread along one raw edge. With right sides together, pin Skirt to bodice. Draw up gathers to fit and stitch, taking care not to catch bodice lining in seam. Turn under raw

edge of bodice lining and slipstitch in place over seam.

Fold Frill in half lengthwise, right sides together, and stitch short ends. Turn right side out and press. Run a gathering thread along raw edge. With right sides together and raw edges even, pin Frill to lower edge of Skirt. Draw up gathers to fit and stitch. Trim and neaten seam.

Cut velvet ribbon in half and thread through broderie anglaise beading, tying in a bow at centre front point. Stitch threaded beading to lower edge of Skirt, concealing Frill seam, turning under ends and stitching to neaten and secure ribbon.

HAT

Tie narrower grosgrain ribbon in a neat bow at front of hat and catch in position with a few stitches. Glue on ribbon roses.

SHOES

Remove buckle and strap from shoes supplied with doll and paint white shoes black. Cut small buttonholes in Shoe Upper, as indicated on pattern, to correspond with size of pearl beads. Glue upper to shoe. Stitch on beads to correspond.

MODERN DOLL'S CLOTHES

Materials

■ 0.2m x 90cm fine white fabric, for bloomers
■ 0.3m x 90cm tartan fabric, for pinafore
■ 40cm square cotton print, for blouse
■ One felt square, for beret
■ Small amount hat elastic, to fit waist and legs
■ Four small wooden beads
■ Six tiny press-studs
■ One small button
■ 0.25m x 1cm-wide tartan ribbon
■ Small ball 8-ply knitting cotton
■ Pair 4mm knitting needles

Pattern pieces

All pattern pieces, except rectangles, are printed on the pattern sheet, Side 4, in black.

Trace Pantaloons Front, Pantaloons Back, Pinafore Bodice Front, Pinafore Bodice Back, Dress/Petticoat Bodice Front, Dress/Petticoat Bodice Back, Sleeve and Collar.

Cutting

Note. 6mm seam allowance is included on all pieces unless otherwise specified.

From white fabric, cut two Pantaloon Fronts and two Pantaloon Backs.

From tartan fabric, cut two Pinafore Bodice Fronts, two Pinafore Bodice Backs and one rectangle, 20cm x 80cm, for Skirt.

From cotton print, cut one Bodice Front (to Edwardian bodice line), two Bodice Backs (note: do not cut Bodice Backs on fold; add 1.5cm seam allowance to fold line and cut two single pieces, to Edwardian bodice line), two Sleeves, four Collars and two rectangles, each 3cm x 6cm, for Cuffs.

From felt, cut one 16cm diameter circle for Crown and one rectangle, 23cm x 2.5cm for Band.

A: Pinafore bodice front.
B: Pantaloons front.
C: Pantaloons back.
D: Dress/ petticoat/Blouse
bodice front.
E: Dress/ petticoat/Blouse
bodice back.
F: Collar.
G: Pinafore bodice back.
H: Sleeve.

Sewing

BLOOMERS

Stitch the Bloomers as for the Pantaloons, on page 61, but instead of the lace beading and lace edging, finish the upper and lower edges with a narrow casing and thread with hat elastic to fit the doll's waist.

PINAFORE

Construct as for Petticoat, on page 61, omitting reference to lace.

Stitch four small wooden beads to centre front and three tiny press-studs to close at centre back.

BLOUSE

With right sides together, join Bodice Front to Backs at shoulders and press seams open.

Neaten raw edges of back opening and turn in on fold line.

With right sides together, stitch Collars together in pairs, leaving neck edge open.

With right sides together and raw edges even, stitch under collars to neck edge of blouse, positioning curved

edge of collars at the centre front. Turn in raw edge on upper collar and slip-stitch over seam.

Gather Sleeve crowns to fit armholes and stitch in place.

Trim and neaten seam. Gather lower edge of Sleeve to fit Cuff and stitch.

With right sides together, stitch front to backs at sides and underarms, continuing across Cuff in one continuous seam. Fold Cuff in half to inside, turn in raw edge and slip-stitch over cuff seam.

Sew button to centre front. Catch Collar to front of blouse on either side of button. Finish lower edge of blouse with a narrow hem.

Lap the Bodice Backs and stitch on the press-studs, positioning the first on top of the collar, keeping it flattened at the back.

BERET

Stitch short ends of Band together (Band should fit around doll's head). Run a gathering thread around outer edge of Crown and draw up gathers to fit Band.

With right sides together and raw edges even, stitch Band to Crown.

Fold Band in half to inside and slip-stitch edge over seam.

Trim edge of beret with tartan ribbon, a felt bow, if desired, and a small tab, rolled from a scrap of felt, approximately 1cm x 3cm.

KNITTED SOCKS (make 2)

Cast on 16sts and work 30 rows of K2/P1 rib.
Row 31. K2 tog to end of row...8sts.
Next and alt row. P to end of row.
Row 33. K2 tog, to end of row...4sts.
Row 35. K2 tog to end of row... 2 sts.
Cast off.

To make up

With right sides facing, stitch sides together to form a close-fitting sock. Turn right side out.

DOLLY KNITS

The best-dressed dolls head for the ski fields with a suitcase full of knitted outfits to warm their winter holidays. Our charming miss is wearing her slimline ski pants and matching jumper, but the fluffy pink lacy number and adorable Fair Isle cardigan and matching pleated skirt are sure to get an airing, aprés ski.

APRÉS SKI WEAR

25 sts and 33 rows to 10cm over st st, using 3.75mm size needles.

SKIRT

(worked in one piece)

Using 3.75mm needles, cast on 152 sts.

1st row. (wrong side). Knit.

2nd row. K6, sl 1 (knitwise), K3, P1, *K10, sl 1 (knitwise), K3, P1; rep from * to last 6 sts, K6.

3rd row. P6, K1, *P14, K1; rep from * to last 10 sts, P10.

Rep 2nd and 3rd rows 15 times more.

Next row. K7, cast off 7 sts, (K8, cast off 7 sts) 9 times, K3...82 sts.

Work 5 rows st st, beg with a purl row and dec 7 sts evenly across last row... 75 sts.

Change to 3mm needles.

Next row. K2, *P1, K1; rep from * to last st, K1.

Next row. K1, *Pl, KI; rep from * to end.

Rep last 2 rows 3 times more.

Cast off loosely in rib.

To make up

Stitch top of pleats closed on wrong side, then catch to Skirt so that pleats sit flat and all in the one direction. Join centre back seam. Thread 3 lengths of round elastic through back of rib rows and waistband and draw up to fit.

CARDIGAN

Body
(worked in one piece to underarm)

Using C2 and and 3mm needles, cast on 81 sts.

1st row. K2, *P1, K1; rep from * to last st, K1.

2nd row. K1, *P1, K1; rep from * to end.

Rep last 2 rows twice more.

Break off C2.

Change to 3.75mm needles.

Note. When working in Fair Isle, carry colour not in use loosely across wrong side of work. Always carry colours to ends of rows, noting that C1 can be passed up along sides of work. Always carry MC above C1 across row.

Using MC, work 2 rows st st.

3rd row. K4 MC, K1 C1, *K5 MC, K1 C1; rep from * to last 4 sts, K4 MC.

Using MC, work 4 rows st st, beg with a purl row.

8th row. P1 MC, P1 C1, *P5 MC, P1 C1; rep from * to last st, P1 MC.

Using MC, work 2 rows st st.

Last 10 rows form spot patt.

Work a further 10 rows spot patt.

Change to 4mm needles.

Next row. K1 C1, K2 MC, K2 C2, K1 MC, K2 C2, *K2 MC, K2 C1, K1 MC, K2 C1, K2 MC, K2 C2, K1 MC, K2 C2; rep from * to last 3 sts, K2 MC, K1 C1.

Next row. P1 MC, P1 C1, P1 MC, P2 C2, P1 MC, P2 C2, *P1 MC, (P1 C1, P2 MC) twice, P1 C1, (P1 MC, P2 C2) twice; rep from * to last 3 sts, P1 MC, P1 C1, P1 MC.

Next row. K1 C2, K1 MC, (K1 C1, K2 MC) twice, *K1 C1, K1 MC, (K2 C2, K1 MC) twice, (K1 C1, K2 MC) twice; rep from * to last 3 sts, K1 C1, K1 MC, K1 C2.

Next row. P1 C2, P2 MC, P2 C1, P1 MC, P2 C1, *P2 MC, P2 C2, P1 MC, P2 C2, P2 MC, P2 C1, P1 MC, P2 C1; rep from * to last 3 sts, P2 MC, P1 C2.

Change to 3.75mm needles.

Break off C2.

Using MC, work 2 rows st st.

Divide for armholes. Next row. K4 MC, K1 C1, (K5 MC, K1 C1) twice, K1 MC, K2tog MC, *turn.*

SLIMLINE SKIRT AND FAIR ISLE CARDIGAN

Measurements

To fit doll: 42cm tall: 25cm at underarm

Materials

■ Cleckheaton Machinewash Crepe 5-ply (50g):
■ Main Colour (MC): one Ball (Skirt) and one ball (Cardigan)
■ First Contrast (C1): small quantity (Cardigan)
■ Second Contrast (C2): small quantity (Cardigan)
■ One pair each 3mm (No 11), 3.75mm (No 9) and 4mm (No 8) knitting needles
■ One stitch-holder
■ Five small buttons
■ Knitter's needle for sewing seams
■ Round elastic

Tension: See Knitting and Crochet Notes on page 120.

Cont throughout in spot patt (as before) on these 19 sts for **Right Front** as folls:

Work 13 rows patt.

Shape neck. Cast off 4 sts at beg of next row...15 sts.

Dec one st at neck edge in next 4 rows...11 sts.

Work 2 rows.

Shape shoulder. Cast off 4 sts at beg of next row and fol alt row.

Work one row.

Cast off rem 3 sts.

With right side facing, join yarn to rem sts, K2 MC, K1 C1, (K5 MC, K1 C1) 6 times, K2 MC, *turn.*

Cont throughout in spot part (as before) on these 41 sts for Back as folls:

Work 19 rows patt.

Shape shoulders. Cast off 4 sts at beg of next 4 rows, then 3 sts at beg of foll 2 rows.

Leave rem 19 sts on stitchholder.

With right side facing, join yarn to rem 20 sts, K2tog MC, K1 MC, K1 C1 (K5 MC, K1 C1) twice, K4 MC.

Cont throughout in spot patt (as before) on these 19 sts for **Left Front** as folls:

Work 13 rows patt.

Shape neck. Next row. Patt to last 4 sts, cast off last 4 sts.

With wrong side facing, rejoin yarn to rem 15 sts and dec one st at neck edge in next 4 rows...11 sts.

Work one row.

Shape shoulder. Complete as for Right Front shoulder.

Sleeves

Using C2 and 3mm needles, cast on 23 sts.

Work 6 rows rib as for Body, inc 2 sts evenly across last row...25 sts.

Break off C2.

Change to 3.75mm needles.

Using MC, work 2 rows st st.

3rd row. K3 MC, K1 C1, (K5 MC, K1 C1) 3 times, K3 MC.

4th row. Using MC, purl. Cont in spot patt as for Body as placed in last 4 rows, AT THE SAME TIME inc one st at each end of next and foll 4th rows until there are 35 sts.

Work a further 9 rows straight in spot patt. Cast off.

Neckband

Join shoulder seams. With right side facing, using C2 and 3mm needles, knit up 49 sts evenly around neck, incl sts from stitchholder.

Work 5 rows rib as for Body, beg with a 2nd row.

Cast off loosely in rib.

Right Front Band

With right side facing, using C2 and 3mm needles, knit up 45 sts evenly along edge of Right Front and across end of Neckband.

Work 2 rows rib as for Body, beg with a 2nd row.

3rd row. Rib 2, yrn, P2tog tbl, (rib 8, yrn, P2tog tbl) 4 times, K1...5 buttonholes.

Work 2 rows rib.

Cast off loosely in rib.

Left Front Band

Work to correspond with Right Front Band, omitting buttonholes.

To make up

Join Sleeve seams. Sew in Sleeves, placing centre of Sleeves to shoulder seams. Sew buttons in position.

DOLL'S SKI PANTS AND JUMPER

Measurements

To fit doll: 42cm tall: 25cm at underarm

Materials

- Cleckheaton Machinewash Crepe 5-ply (50g):
- One ball navy (Pants)
- One ball cream (Jumper)
- One pair each 3.75mm (No 9) and 3mm (No 11) knitting needles
- Two small buttons (Jumper)
- Knitter's needle for seams

Tension: See Knitting and Crochet Notes on page 120.

25 sts and 33 rows to 10cm over st st, using 3.75mm needles.

Special abbreviations: M1: make one st (pick up loop which lies before next st, place it on lefthand needle and knit into back of loop).

Traditional Cast-On Method

Cut a 1.5m length of yarn and double. Make a slip knot on knitting needle using main ball of yarn. Hold double yarn in left hand and wind twice (anti-clockwise) around left thumb. With needle in right hand, insert needle from bottom to top under 4 strands. Using main ball of yarn, knit a st, slipping 4 strands off thumb. Pull double yarn firmly to complete knot. Then yfwd (to make a st). You should now have 3 sts on needle. Again wind double yarn around thumb and knit a st, then yfwd. Cont to cast on in this manner until you have required number of sts.

PANTS

Left leg

(beg at ankle)

Using 3mm needles, cast on 29sts.

1st row. K2, *P1, K1; rep from * to last st, K1.

2nd row. K1, *P1, K1; rep from * to end.

Rep 1st and 2nd rows once more.

Change to 3.75mm needles.

Work 2 rows st st.

3rd row. K2, M1, knit to last 2 sts, M1, K2.

Cont in st st, inc one st (as before) at each end of foll 6th rows until there are 39 sts, then in alt rows until there are 45 sts. Work one row.

Shape crotch. Cast off 2 sts at beg of next 2 rows...41 sts.

Cont in st st, dec one st at each end of next and foll alt rows until 35 sts rem.** Work 19 rows st st.

Note. When turning when shaping back, bring yarn to front of work, sl next st on righthand needle, ybk, sl st back on to lefthand needle, then turn and proceed as instructed, to avoid making holes in work.

Shape back. 1st row. K16, *turn.*

2nd and alt rows. Purl to end.

3rd row. K11, *turn.*

5th row. K6, *turn.*

7th row. Knit across all sts to end.

8th row. Purl.

Change to 3mm needles. Work 6 rows in rib (as before).

Cast off loosely in rib.

Right leg

(beg at ankle)

Work as for left leg to **

Work 20 rows st st.

Shape back. 1st row. P16, *turn.*

2nd and alt rows. Knit to end.

3rd row. P11, *turn.*

5th row. P6, *turn.*

7th row. Purl across all sts to end.

Change to 3mm needles.

Work 6 rows in rib (as before).

Cast off loosely in rib.

Foot Strap (make 2)

Using 3.00mm needles, cast on 21sts.

Work 2 rows rib, as for Left Leg.

Cast off loosely in rib.

To make up

Join centre front and back seams. Join inside leg seams. Sew foot straps in position. If desired, thread lengths of round elastic through back of rib rows at waist and draw up to fit.

JUMPER

Back and Front (alike)

Using 3.75mm needles, cast on 38 sts using the Traditional Cast-On Method. Knit 8 rows garter st.

Next row. K2, *P2, K2; rep from * to end.

Next row. P2, *K2, P2; rep from * to end.

Rep last 2 rows twice more.

Work 22 rows st st.

Tie a marker at each end of last row to mark beg of armholes as there is no armhole shaping.

Work a further 8 rows st st.

Note. When turning when shaping neck, bring yarn to front of work, sl next st on righthand needle, ybk, sl st back on to lefthand needle, then turn and proceed as instructed, to avoid making holes in work.

Shape neck. 1st row. K15, *turn*.
2nd and alt rows. Knit to end.
3rd row. K13, *turn*.
5th row. K11, *turn*.
7th row. Knit across all sts to end.
Proceed as folls:
1st row. P15, *turn*.
2nd and alt rows. Purl to end.
3rd row. P13, *turn*.
5th row. P11, *turn*.
7th row. Purl across all sts to end...38sts.
Knit 6 rows garter st. Cast off.

Sleeves

Using 3mm needles, cast on 22 sts.
Work 6 rows rib as for Back and Front, inc 4 sts evenly across last row...26 sts.
Change to 3.75mm needles.
Work 2 rows st st.
3rd row. K2, M1, knit to last 2 sts, M1, K2.
Cont in st st, inc one st (as before) at each end of foll 4th rows until there are 34 sts.
Work a further 3 rows st st.
Work 6 rows rib as before.
Cast off loosely in rib.

To make up

Join shoulders for 4 sts each side of neck at armhole edge. Sew in Sleeves between markers, placing centre of Sleeves to shoulder seams.
Join side and Sleeve seams. Attach the button and buttonloop (made as desired) to each side of neck and fasten.

DOLL'S LACY JUMPER

Measurements

To fit doll: 42cm tall: 25cm at underarm

Materials

Panda Souffle 8-ply (50g):
■ Two balls
■ One pair each 3.25mm (No 10) and 4mm (No 8) knitting needles

■ Two large safety pins
■ Three small buttons
■ Knitter's needle for sewing seams

Tension: See **Knitting and Crochet Notes** on page 120.
22 sts and 30 rows to 10cm over st st, using 4mm needles.

Back and Front (alike)

Using 3.25mm needles, cast on 39 sts.
1st row. K2, *P1, K1; rep from * to last st, K1.
2nd row. K1, *P1, K1; rep from * to end.
Rep 1st and 2nd rows twice more.
Change to 4mm needles.
Beg Patt. 1st row. K2 *yfwd, sl 1, K1, psso, K3, yfwd, sl 1, K1, psso, K2, K2tog, yfwd, K1; rep from * to last st, K1.
2nd row. Purl.
3rd row. K2, *yfwd, sl 1, K1, psso, K1, K2tog, yfwd, K1, yfwd, sl 1, K1, psso, K1, K2tog, yfwd, K1; rep from * to last st, K1.
4th row. Purl.
5th row. K2, *yfwd, sl 1, K1, psso, K2tog, yfwd, K3, yfwd, sl 1, K1 psso, K2tog, yfwd, K1; rep from * to last st, K1.
6th row. Purl.
Rows 1 to 6 incl form patt. Work a further 12 rows patt. Tie a marker at each end of last row to mark beg of armholes as there is no armhole shaping. Work 12 rows patt.
Shape neck. Next row. Patt 16, *turn*. Cont on these 16 sts.
Keeping patt correct, dec one st at end of alt rows until 13 sts rem. Work one row. Cast off.
With right side facing, sl next 7 sts on safety pin and leave.
Join yarn to rem 16 sts and patt to end of row.
Keeping patt correct, dec one st at beg of alt rows until 13 sts rem.
Work one row. Cast off.

Sleeves

Using 3.25mm needles, cast on 21 sts.
Work 6 rows rib as for Back and Front, inc 6 sts evenly across last row...27sts.
Change to 4mm needles.

Work 18 rows patt as for Back and Front. Cast off loosely.

Neckband

Join right shoulder seam. With right side facing and using 3.25mm needles, knit up 39 sts evenly around neck, incl sts from safety pins.
Work 3 rows rib as for Back and Front, beg with a 2nd row.
Cast off loosely in rib.

To make up

Join left shoulder seam at armhole edge for 4 sts. Sew in Sleeves between markers, placing centre of Sleeves to shoulder seams.
Join side and Sleeve seams.
Attach buttonloops (made as desired) and buttons to shoulder openings and fasten.

BARBIE'S BRIDE'S DRESS

Measurements

Dress designed to fit Barbie® or any 29cm teen doll.

Materials

- 0.3m x 90cm shantung fabric (silk polyester etc)
- 0.3m x 90cm sheer embroidered fabric
- 0.2m x 90cm organza lining
- 0.6m x 100cm net
- 0.4m x l50cm tulle
- 1.3m x 1cm-wide lace edging
- Three small hooks and eyes
- 0.2m x 4mm-wide elastic
- Pearl spray for headpiece
- Small artificial flowers for bouquet
- 0.5m x 55mm-wide satin ribbon
- Pearl-headed pins to fix veil

Pattern pieces

Pattern pieces are printed on the pattern sheet, Side 1, in black. Trace Front Bodice 111, Back Bodice 112 and Sleeve 115.

Cutting

Note. Remember to **add** 1cm seam allowance to all pieces, except to upper and lower edges of Front and Back Bodices, and centre back edge of Back Bodice, (already included).

There is also no need to add an allowance to lower edge of Sleeve, as this will be finished with lace. All the following rectangle measurements already include seam allowances.

From shantung, cut one Front Bodice, two Back Bodices, one 21cm x 57cm rectangle for skirt and one 3cm x 12cm strip for waistband. From shantung scraps, cut bias strips to make a fabric bow.

From sheer embroidered fabric, cut one Front Bodice, two Back Bodices, two Sleeves and one 21cm x 57cm rectangle for overskirt.

From organza lining, cut two Sleeves, one 21cm x 57cm skirt and one 5cm x 25cm strip for yoke of net underskirt.

From net, cut two 30cm x 100cm rectangles for underskirt.

Sewing

Bodice and skirt are separate garments. Baste shantung and sheer embroidered fabric Bodice sections to one another, wrong side of sheer fabric facing right side of shantung. Baste Sleeve linings to Sleeves, wrong sides together. Having "mounted" the pieces together in this way, treat them as a single layer for sewing.

Sew darts in Bodice Fronts. With right sides together, stitch side seams. Trim and neaten seam.

Press under hem allowance on top edge of Bodice and either topstitch or slip-stitch in place. Turn in facing allowance along fold line on centre back edges and top-stitch or slip-stitch in place. Turn up and sew a narrow hem on lower edge of bodice. Sew on fasteners to centre back.

Cut two pieces of lace edging to fit along lower edge of Sleeve. Position lace over raw edges of Sleeve and stitch in place with narrow zigzag stitch. Gather top edge of Sleeves, between dots.

With right sides together, stitch Sleeve seams and trim.

Sew Sleeves by hand to top edge of Bodice, matching seams and small dots. Pull up gathers to fit over the shoulders of the doll, turn under seam allowance and sew neatly by hand with ends of gathering thread, to hold gathers in position.

By hand, run a row of gathering around lower edge of Sleeve, as indicated on pattern, to make a frill. Draw up gathers to fit arm (but not too tightly) and fasten off.

To make net underskirt, fold each rectangle in half lengthwise and sew short edges to each other with a narrow zigzag stitch, forming two circles. Place one circle inside the other, with all raw edges even, and run two rows of gathering threads around edge.

With right sides together, stitch together short ends of organza under-skirt yoke. Stitch a narrow casing along one long edge of yoke.

Draw up gathers of net underskirt to fit lower edge of yoke and, with right sides together, stitch yoke to under-skirt. Trim seam and neat-en with a zigzag stitch. Insert elastic into casing to fit waist and secure ends.

To make skirt, stitch centre back seam in each of shantung and lining skirt rectangles, leaving 5cm unsewn for back opening. Press seams open.

With right sides facing,

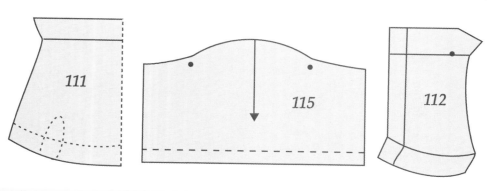

BARBIE DAZZLER!

Since the first Barbie® doll first appeared in toy shops more than 30 years ago, she has proved a never-ending source of enjoyment to generations of children devoted to the former fashion model and her seemingly endless wardrobe of clothes. Now you can add to your own Barbie's wardrobe with our super collection of garments with everything a well-dressed doll could possibly wish for, from underwear and nightclothes through casual outfits and sportswear to designer evening clothes ... and even a wedding dress!

sew lining and skirt together around hem edge. Turn right side out and press.

Turn in seam allowance on back opening edges and slip-stitch folded edges to one another.

Fold sheer embroidered overskirt in half crosswise, right sides together, and slash along fold line to a depth of about 4.5cm. Sew a 1cm-wide dart below slash, tapering it away to nothing. Hand-sew a narrow hem on either side of slash.

Round the front edges of the overskirt by removing lower corners and cutting towards waist in a graceful curve. Attach lace edging around curved edges and along hem of overskirt. Place overskirt over the shantung underskirt, matching centre fronts and backs, and baste raw edges together. Run a gathering thread around upper edge and draw up gathers to fit waist.

With right sides together, stitch one long side of waistband to the skirt, extending end a little to form tab for fastener. Press under remaining raw edge of waistband and slip-stitch in place over waistband seam. Neaten centre back edges of waistband. Sew on hook and eye.

From scraps of shantung, make a fabric bow with long ties and attach to waistband at centre back.

Round the corners of the tulle rectangle. Fold back a section large enough to form a face veil (about 14cm) and gather folded edge onto the pearl spray, to form hairpiece and veil. Fix veil to hair with pearl-headed pins.

Make bouquet from small artificial flowers, allowing one wire stalk to protrude at back for attaching to bride's hand. Back flowers with a little tulle frill and add narrow ribbon to decorate.

BARBIE BRIDESMAID DRESS

Measurements

Dress designed to fit Barbie or any 29cm teen doll.

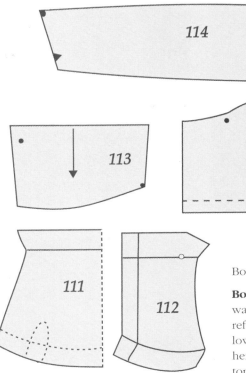

Materials

■ 0.2m x 112cm paper taffeta
■ 0.1m x 150cm tulle
■ Three small hooks and eyes
■ Small artificial flowers for bouquet and hairpiece
■ 1m x 3mm-wide ribbon

Pattern pieces

Pattern pieces are printed on the pattern sheet, Side 1, in black. Trace Front Bodice 111, Back Bodice 112, Skirt 113, Skirt Frill 114 and Sleeve 115.

Cutting

Note. Remember to *add* 1cm seam allowance to all pieces, except to upper and lower edges of Front and Back Bodices, and centre back edge of Back Bodice, (allowances included).

From paper taffeta, cut one Front Bodice, two Back Bodices, one Skirt, one Skirt Frill, two Sleeves and one waistband, 11.5cm x 3cm. From taffeta scraps, cut bias strips to make a sash and fabric bow for waist, if desired.

From tulle, cut two Skirt Frills.

Sewing

Bodice and skirt are separate garments.

Bodice: Construct bodice in the same way as Bride's dress, ignoring the references to "mounting", and finishing lower edges of Sleeves with a narrow hem instead of lace. Top-stitch around top edge of bodice, if desired.

Skirt: With right sides together, stitch centre front seam of both tulle and taffeta Skirt Frills. Turn under and sew a narrow hem on lower edge of taffeta Frill. Pin the two tulle Frills to the wrong side of the taffeta Frill, baste raw edges together and run two rows of gathering around edge, through all layers. Trim tulle if it extends below Frill.

With right sides together, stitch centre back seam of Skirt, as far as opening. Press under seam allowance on opening edges and hem narrowly.

Run a gathering thread around top edge of Skirt and draw up gathers to fit waist. With right sides together, stitch Skirt to Waistband, extending one end of waistband as an underlap. Press under remaining raw edges of waistband and slipstitch in place over waistband seam. Top-stitch waistband close to seam.

Pull up gathering thread on Skirt Frill to fit Skirt. With right sides together, stitch Frill to Skirt. Trim and neaten seam. Sew on a hook and eye at the waistband.

Make a sash and fabric bow with trailing ties for centre back, if desired, or fashion a sash from purchased ribbon. Make a small bouquet of flowers and decorate with tulle and ribbon loops.

General instructions

■ All garments to fit a Barbie® or any 29cm teen doll.
■ Remember to add 5mm seam allowance to all pattern pieces before cutting.
■ Specific fabric amounts are not given as most garments can be constructed from small scraps.
■ To prevent fraying, it is advisable to finish edges of each pattern piece with a small, narrow zigzag stitch.
■ Unless otherwise indicated, pieces are stitched together with right sides facing.
■ When elastic is required, use a flat, narrow lingerie elastic. Lay elastic along seamline on wrong side of fabric and secure with a narrow zigzag, stretching elastic to fit across pattern piece. Fold to inside along stitching line.

STRETCH BRA AND KNICKERS

Materials

■ Scrap of white knit fabric
■ Small amount 3mm lace
■ Narrow lingerie elastic
■ Velcro

Pattern pieces

All pattern pieces are printed on the pattern sheet, Side 1, in red. Trace Bra Front/Back 1 and Knickers Front/Back 2.

DRESSING UP BARBIE

Cutting

Note. Remember to *add* 5mm seam allowance to all pieces.

From knit fabric, cut one Bra and one Knickers.

Sewing

Bra: Stitch darts in centre front. Fold neck and armhole edges to inside and top-stitch in place 2mm from edge, taking care not to stretch fabric as you stitch.

Stitch side seams.

Apply the elastic to the lower edge as described under *General Instructions.* Fold elastic to the inside, slip edge of lace under edge of Bra, right sides facing you, and stitch close to folded edge of Bra.

Fold seam allowance at centre back to inside and stitch 2mm from edge. Cut a small piece of Velcro, 3.5cm x 1cm, and stitch to edges of centre back.

Knickers: Apply elastic and lace to upper edge of Knickers, as for Bra. Stitch centre back seam.

Finish leg edges as for neck and armhole edges of Bra.

Stitch crotch seam.

BRA & BOXER SHORTS

Materials

- Scrap of checked fabric
- 0.3m narrow broderie anglaise
- 0.3m x 2mm-wide ribbon
- Narrow lingerie elastic
- Velcro

Pattern pieces

All pattern pieces are printed on the pattern sheet, Side 1, in red. Trace Bra

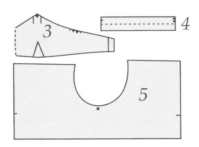

Front/Back 3, Strap 4 and Boxer Shorts Front/Back 5.

Cutting

Note. Remember to *add* 5mm seam allowance to all pieces.

From checked fabric, cut one Bra, two Straps and two Shorts Front/Backs.

Sewing

Bra: Stitch darts in centre front. Press under seam allowance on upper and lower edge and stitch in place, 2mm from edge. Clip to stitching at centre front point.

Press under seam allowance on edges of Straps, fold each Strap in half lengthwise, wrong sides together, and top-stitch long edges. Place in position, matching symbols, and stitch in place.

Fold under seam allowance at centre back edges and top-stitch 2mm from edge. Cut a 1cm square of Velcro and

stitch securely to centre back edges.

Boxer Shorts: With the right sides together and raw edges even, stitch lace to lower edge of Shorts. Press lace downwards and press seam away from lace. Top-stitch 5mm above seam.

Stitch side seams, leaving open below split symbol. Fold seam allowances of split to inside and top-stitch around split, 2mm from edge.

Pin and stitch crotch seam. Finish upper edge with elastic as described under the *General Instructions*.

Cut ribbon into three pieces, tie each into a tiny bow and stitch to Shorts, and Bra, as pictured.

NIGHTIE

Materials

- Scrap of nightdress fabric
- One tiny button
- Machine thread in contrast colour

Pattern pieces

All pattern pieces are printed on the pattern sheet, Side 1, in red. Trace Nightie Front 6, Nightie Back 7 and Shoulder Strap 8.

Cutting

Note. Remember to **add** 5mm seam allowance to all pieces.

From nightdress fabric, cut two Fronts, two Backs and two Shoulder Straps.

Sewing

Stitch centre front seam of Fronts. Stitch darts in Fronts.

Stitch centre back seam, leaving open above split symbol.

Stitch front to back at side seams, leaving open below split symbols.

Press under seam allowance on top edge and top-stitch 2mm from edge. Clip in towards stitching at centre front.

Press under seam allowance on edges of Straps, fold each Strap in half lengthwise, wrong sides together, and top-stitch long edges.

Place the straps in position, matching symbols, and stitch in place at the front and back.

Press under seam allowance at centre back split and topstitch 2mm from edge. Make a tiny thread loop between the symbols at top edge of centre back and sew on a tiny button to correspond.

Fold hem allowance to inside and pin. Work decorative machine-stitching along given line so that hem is secured.

Press seam allowances on split edges to inside and topstitch 2mm from edge.

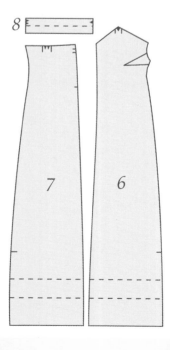

BODY SUIT

Materials

- Scrap of knit fabric
- 0.1m x 2mm-wide ribbon
- Velcro

Pattern pieces

Pattern piece is printed on pattern sheet, Side 1, in red. Trace Body Suit Front/Back 9.

Cutting

Note. Remember to **add** 5mm seam allowance to all pieces. Fold fabric double, cut 1 Front/Back on fold, then cut centre back split to symbol.

Sewing

Stitch the front to the back at shoulders.

Fold seam allowance of neck edge to inside and top-stitch 2mm from edge, taking care not to stretch fabric as you work. Finish sleeve and leg edges in the same manner. Stitch side seams.

Fold narrow hem to inside at centre back and top-stitch 2mm from edge. Cut a piece of Velcro, 5cm x 0.5cm, and stitch in place at opening. Close Velcro and reinforce lower edge of the opening with a couple of zigzag stitches.

Tie a tiny ribbon bow and stitch in place at centre front.

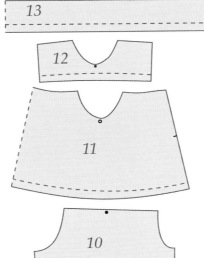

BABY DOLL PYJAMAS

Materials

- Scrap of floral print
- One tiny button
- Narrow lingerie elastic

Pattern pieces

All the pattern pieces are printed on the pattern sheet, Side 1, in red. Trace Baby Doll Pants Front/Back 10, Top Front/Back 11, Sleeve 12 and Collar 13.

Cutting

Note. Remember to **add** 5mm seam allowance to all pieces.

From floral print, cut two Pants Front/Backs, one Top Front/Back, two Sleeves and one Collar.

Sewing

Top: Stitch Sleeves to Front/Back at armholes. Press under a narrow hem on lower edge of Sleeves and stitch. Stitch front to back at shoulders.

Press under seam allowance on one long edge of Collar and topstitch 2mm from edge. Pin Collar to neck edge of top. Apply the elastic to the neck edge, as described under the **General Instructions**. Fold elastic to inside along stitching and top-stitch it in place, stretching as you stitch.

Stitch centre back seam below split symbol. Press under seam allowance on split edges and top-stitch 2mm from edge.

Work a small thread loop between symbols at centre back neck edge and sew on a tiny button to correspond.

Press under a narrow hem on lower edge and stitch.

Pants: Apply elastic to upper and lower edges, as for neck edge of Top. Stitch inside leg seams, then centre front/back seam.

PYJAMAS

Materials

- Checked fabric
- Three tiny buttons
- Three tiny press-studs
- Narrow lingerie elastic

Pattern pieces

All pattern pieces are printed on the pattern sheet, Side 1, in red. Trace Jacket Front 14, Pocket 15, Jacket Back 16, Sleeve 17, Collar 18 and Pants Front/Back 19.

Cutting

Note. Remember to **add** 5mm seam allowance to all pieces.

From checked fabric, cut two Jacket Fronts, two Pockets, one Jacket Back, two Sleeves, one Collar and two Pants Front/Backs.

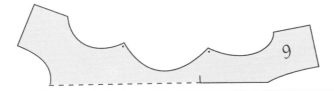

Stitch the Fronts to the Back at the shoulders.

Fold Collar along fold line, right sides together, and stitch side edges. Turn Collar right side out and stitch one edge of Collar to neck edge of jacket.

Fold jacket front facing to outside along fold line, right sides together, sandwiching Collar, and stitch. Turn facing back to inside, fold under seam allowance on remaining edge of the Collar and slip-stitch in place over seam.

Stitch Sleeves to armholes of jacket. Press under a narrow hem on lower edge of Sleeves and stitch.

Stitch Sleeve and side seams in one operation, leaving open below split symbols.

Press under a narrow hem on lower edge of jacket, opening out front facing. Stitch in place, then fold front facing back to inside and catch in place.

Press under seam allowance on split edges and top-stitch 2mm from edge.

Sew tiny buttons to the right front and stitch press-studs beneath them to secure the front opening.

Pants: Press under hem allowance on lower edges of pants and top-stitch 2mm from edge.

Stitch side seams, then centre front/back seam.

Apply elastic to the upper edge as described under the *General Instructions.* Fold elastic to inside along the stitching and stitch in place, stretching as you stitch.

Pattern pieces

All pattern pieces are printed on pattern sheet, Side 1, in red. Trace Teddy Front/Back 20 and Shoulder Strap 21.

Cutting

Note. Remember to *add* 5mm seam allowance to all pieces. From floral print, cut two Front/Backs and two Shoulder Straps.

Sewing

Press under a narrow hem on lower edge of legs and stitch.

Stitch side seams above the split symbols.

Press under seam allowance on split edges and top-stitch 2mm from edge.

Stitch centre front/back seam, leaving open above split symbol at centre back.

Pin elastic along given line on wrong side of the garment, anchor one end firmly, then zigzag in place, stretching to fit as you stitch.

Press under seam allowance on

Sewing

Jacket: Fold Pocket facing to outside along fold line and stitch side edges. Turn facing back to inside and press under remaining raw edges of Pocket. Stitch across upper edge 5mm from top. Repeat for remaining Pocket. Top-stitch Pockets in place on Jacket Front.

TEDDY

Materials

- Floral print fabric
- One tiny button
- Narrow lingerie elastic
- 0.3m x 2mm-wide ribbon

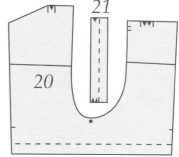

upper edge and top-stitch 2mm from the edge.

Press under seam allowance on centre back split edges and top-stitch 2mm from edge. Work a tiny thread loop between symbols at centre back and sew on button to correspond.

Press under seam allowances on Shoulder Straps, then fold Straps in half lengthwise, wrong sides facing. Top-stitch along both long edges. Stitch Straps in place at front and back, following symbols.

Cut ribbon into four equal lengths, tie each into a tiny bow and stitch one above each split and the remaining two to front of Teddy, as photographed.

DRESSING GOWN & SLIPPERS

Materials

■ Waffle-weave cotton
■ Small amount iron-on interfacing

Pattern pieces

All pattern pieces are printed on the pattern sheet, Side 1, in red. Trace Front 22, Front/Neck Binding 23, Pocket 24, Back 25, Sleeve 26, Tie 27, Slipper Upper 122 and Slipper Sole 123.

Cutting

Note. Remember to *add* 5mm seam allowance to all pieces, except Slipper pieces, which are cut without seam allowance.

From waffle-weave cotton, cut two Fronts, one Front/Neck Binding, one Pocket, one Back, two Sleeves, one Tie, four Slipper Uppers and four Slipper Soles.

From interfacing, cut four Slipper Uppers and four Slipper Soles.

Sewing

Dressing Gown: Fold Pocket facing to outside along fold line, right sides together, and stitch along front edge of

facing. Fold facing back to inside and topstitch 1cm from upper edge. Press under seam allowance on front and lower edge of Pocket, then top-stitch Pocket in place on the right Front, matching raw side edges.

Stitch Fronts to Back at shoulders.

Fold lower edge of Sleeves to inside

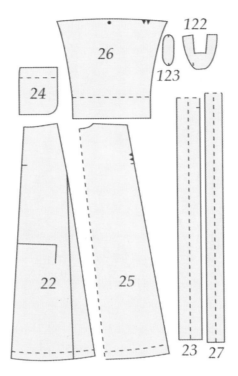

along fold line and stitch. Stitch Sleeves to armholes. Fold cuffs to outside on lower Sleeves and pin to hold.

Stitch Sleeve and side seams in one continuous operation, securing cuffs at the same time.

Press under a narrow hem on lower edge and stitch.

With right sides together, stitch one long side of Front/Neck Binding to raw edge of gown. Press under seam allowance on remaining raw edge of binding, fold binding in half to inside and slip-stitch pressed edge over seam.

Fold Tie in half lengthwise, right sides together and stitch, leaving a small opening for turning. Turn right side out and top-stitch around all edges.

Slipper pieces: With wrong sides facing, stitch pieces together in pairs around outer edges, using a close, narrow zigzag stitch. Stitch centre back seam by hand, then attach Uppers to Soles, also by hand.

Slippers can also be made from felt, using just one layer of felt and no interfacing.

CYCLING OUTFIT

Materials

- Black and yellow jersey knit
- 0.2m each narrow black and white braid
- Narrow lingerie elastic
- Velcro

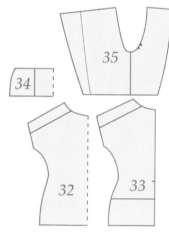

Pattern pieces

All pattern pieces are printed on the pattern sheet, Side 1, in black. Trace Shirt Front 32, Shirt Back 33, Back Pocket 34 and Shorts Front/Back 35.

Cutting

Note. Remember to **add** 5mm seam allowance to all pieces.

From yellow knit fabric, cut one Shirt Front, two Shirt Backs and one Back Pocket.

From black knit fabric, cut two Shorts Front/Backs.

Sewing

Shirt: Stitch the centre back seam, leaving open above split symbol.

Fold under seam allowance on upper edge of Back Pocket and top-stitch 2mm from edge. Place Pocket in position on Back, matching lower and side edges, and make vertical lines of stitching, as given.

Stitch the Front to the Back at the shoulders. Place black braid along given lines on front and back and top-stitch in place.

Turn under seam allowance on neck and armhole edges and top-stitch 2mm from the edge, taking care not to stretch fabric as you stitch.

Turn under seam allowance on the centre back split and top-stitch 2mm from edge. Cut a piece of Velcro, 2cm x 0.5cm and stitch to edges of split to secure opening.

Stitch side seams, sandwiching side edges of Back Pocket at the same time.

Fold the seam allowance on lower edge to inside (including lower edge of the Back Pocket) and stitch.

Shorts: Place white braid along given lines on Shorts front; top-stitch in place. Fold under seam allowance on lower edges and top-stitch 2mm from edge.

Stitch back seams. Pin inside leg seams and stitch.

Apply elastic to upper edge of Shorts, as described under the **General Instructions,** page 76.

BALLET OUTFIT

Materials

- Silver stretch lamé
- Silver bias binding
- Small amount of tulle
- Velcro

Pattern pieces

All pattern pieces are printed on the pattern sheet, Side 1, in black. Trace Leotard Front/Back 28, Leotard Strap 29, Detachable Quarter Skirt 30 and Waistband 31.

Cutting

Note. Remember to **add** 5mm seam allowance to all pieces.

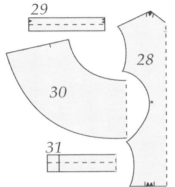

From stretch lamé, cut one Front/Back and two Shoulder Straps.

From tulle, cut two Skirts (on the fold).

From bias binding, cut one Waistband.

Sewing

Leotard: Press under seam allowance around leg edges and top-stitch 2mm from edge. Finish upper edges of front and back in the same way, clipping in to stitching at centre front point.

Stitch side seams.

Fold under seam allowance on Shoulder Straps, then fold each Strap in half lengthwise, wrong sides facing, and topstitch both long edges. Stitch Straps to leotard, following symbols on back and front.

Detachable Skirt: Stitch Skirt sections together at the sides, leaving one side open above split symbol. Fold the bias binding in half, wrong sides facing, enclosing lower edge of Skirt, and stitch in place.

Run a line of small hand stitches around upper edge of Skirt to gather. Pin one edge of Waistband to Skirt, pull up gathers to fit and stitch. Fold remaining edge of Waistband to inside and slip-stitch over seam.

Stitch a 5mm square of Velcro to ends of Waistband to secure.

TENNIS OUTFIT

Materials

- Scraps of white jersey knit
- Scrap of white cotton fabric
- Red felt
- Red, yellow and blue bias binding
- Scrap of double-sided interfacing (optional)
- Velcro

Pattern pieces

All pattern pieces are printed on the pattern sheet, Side 1, in black. Trace Blazer Back 36, Pocket 37, Appliqué B 38, Blazer Front 39, Sleeve 40, Shirt Front/Back 41, Skirt Front/Back 42 and Waistband 43.

Cutting

Note. Remember to **add** 5mm seam allowance to all pieces.

From white jersey, cut one Blazer Back, two Pockets, two Blazer Fronts, two Sleeves and one Shirt Front/Back.

From white cotton, cut two Skirt Front/Backs and one Waistband.

Apply double-sided interfacing to red felt (if using) and cut one Appliqué B, **without seam allowance.**

Sewing

Blazer: Bind top edge of Pockets with yellow bias binding, folding binding in half, enclosing raw edge of Pocket and top-stitching in place.

Press under remaining raw edges of Pockets, and top-stitch Pockets in place on Blazer Fronts.

Stitch Fronts to Back at shoulders.

Bind lower edge of Sleeves with blue

bias binding, as for Pockets. Stitch Sleeves to the armholes of Blazer.

Stitch Sleeve and side seams in one continuous operation.

Finish opening and lower edges of blazer with red bias binding, as for Pockets.

Apply applique B on right Blazer Front using tiny handstitching or double-sided interfacing.

Shirt: Bind armholes of Shirt with bias binding (one red, one blue), following instructions as for Pockets of Blazer.

Stitch shoulder seams and finish the neck edge with bias binding, as before.

Stitch centre back seam, leaving open above split symbol. Fold under split seam allowance and stitch. Cut a 1cm piece of Velcro and stitch to neck edges of split.

Press under seam allowance on lower edge and top-stitch 2mm from edge.

Skirt: Stitch Skirts together at right side seam only. Press under seam allowance on lower edge of Skirt and topstitch 2mm from edge.

Form pleats in waist edge of Skirt, placing symbol X on symbol O. Stitch along top edge to hold.

Stitch remaining side seam, leaving open above split symbol. Press under underlap on one side and baste.

Fold Waistband in half lengthwise, right sides together, and stitch sides. Turn right side out.

Stitch one long edge of Waistband to Skirt, fold under remaining raw edge and slipstitch in place over seam.

Cut a 1cm square of Velcro and attach it to each end of the Waistband.

HIKING OUTFIT

Materials

- Green quilted fabric (see Note)
- Lining
- Striped jersey knit
- Plain ribbed knit (for cuffs)
- Narrow lingerie elastic
- Velcro

Note. If you find it difficult to find suitable fabric, you can quilt your own scrap, using green fabric and thin wadding.

Doing it yourself enables you to machine-quilt the piece in proportion to Barbie's size.

Pattern pieces

All pattern pieces are printed on the pattern sheet, Side 1, in black. Trace Pants Front/Back 19, Sleeveless Vest Front/Back 44, Pocket Flap 45, Front Placket 46 and Collar 47.

Cutting

Note. Remember to *add* 5mm seam allowance to all pieces.

For the outside of the vest, piece 44 is cut in two parts.

From quilted fabric, cut one upper section, on the fold, and one lower section, on the fold, taking care to add seam allowance to edges of both sections. Cut also two Pocket Flaps,

one Front Placket and one Collar.

From lining, cut one complete piece 44.

From striped jersey, cut two Pants Front/Backs.

From plain rib, cut two Cuffs, each 3cm x 6cm.

Sewing

Sleeveless Vest: Fold Pocket Flaps in half along fold lines and stitch around side and curved edges.

Turn right side out and baste in position on lower edge of each upper front section.

Stitch upper and lower sections together, sandwiching Pocket Flaps at

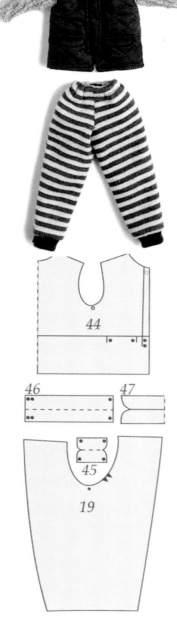

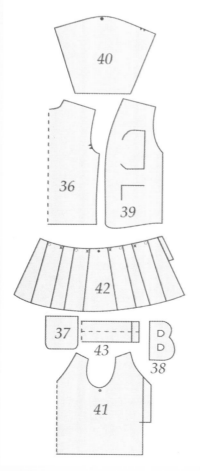

the same time. Press seam allowance upwards and top-stitch close to seam.

With right sides together, stitch lining to vest around front and lower edges, and armholes.

Pull right side out through one shoulder and top-stitch close to the finished edges.

Stitch shoulder seams of vest only (taking care not to catch lining).

Turn under raw edges on lining shoulders and slip-stitch them together.

Fold Front Placket in half lengthwise, right sides together, and stitch across short ends.

Turn right side out. Fold in seam allowance on remaining long sides and baste edges together. Position Placket on right front of the vest, following symbols, and topstitch around all edges of Placket to secure.

Fold Collar in half lengthwise, right sides together and stitch side and curved edges. Turn right side out. Stitch one edge of Collar to neck edge of vest, turn under remaining raw edge and slip-stitch over seam.

Cut a piece of Velcro, 8cm x 1cm, and stitch this under Front Placket and to left side of vest to correspond.

Pants: Fold each ribbing Cuff in half lengthwise, wrong sides together, and stitch to lower edge of the Pants, stretching ribbing to fit.

Stitch side seams. Pin, then stitch centre front/back seam.

Apply the elastic to the waist edge, as described under the **General Instructions,** page 76.

SKI OUTFIT

Materials

- ■ Checked fabric
- ■ Thin wadding
- ■ Scrap of red fabric, for pocket flaps
- ■ Scrap of green fabric, for Hood lining
- ■ Scrap of green jersey or felt
- ■ Smallest possible zip
- ■ Scrap of imitation fur
- ■ Narrow lingerie elastic
- ■ Velcro

Pattern pieces

All pattern pieces are printed on the pattern sheet, Side 1, in black. Trace Ski Suit Front 48, Front Placket 49, Pocket 50, Pocket Flap 51, Ski Suit Back 52, Sleeve 53, Hood 54 and Mitten 124.

Cutting

Note. Remember to **add** 5mm seam allowance to all pieces.

From checked fabric, cut two Ski Suit Fronts, one Front Placket, two Pockets, two Ski Suit Backs, two Sleeves and two Hoods.

From thin wadding, cut two Ski Suit Fronts, two Ski Suit Backs, two Sleeves and two Hoods.

From green fabric, cut two Hoods.

From red fabric, cut two Pocket Flaps.

From green jersey or felt, cut four Mittens, without adding seam allowance.

Sewing

Ski Suit: Baste the wadding sections to the wrong side of the relevant fabric sections.

Press under seam allowance on lower edge of Sleeves, then fold again on facing line, and stitch, creating a narrow casing. Thread elastic through casing and fasten ends securely.

Stitch Fronts to Backs at shoulders. Stitch Sleeves to armholes.

Stitch the Sleeve and side seams in one continuous operation.

Fold Pocket facings to outside along fold line and stitch side edges.

Fold facings back to inside.

Press under remaining raw edges on Pockets.

Attach a 1cm piece of Velcro to upper edge of each Pocket, then position Pockets on Ski Suit, as shown, and top-stitch them in place.

Fold Pocket Flaps in half, right sides together, and stitch side edges.

Turn right side out and attach a 1cm piece of Velcro to centre of each. Position Flaps above Pockets (inside edge of Flap facing you), and stitch close to the raw edge. Fold Flap closed and stitch again, close to seam.

Make casings in the lower edge of the legs, as for Sleeves, and thread with elastic.

Stitch inside leg seams. Stitch centre front/back seam from upper edge of centre back to zip symbol at centre front. Position elastic on given line on inside of suit, secure end, then zigzag in place, stretching elastic to fit as you stitch.

Cut off excess length from lower end of zip and work a few stitches over teeth to secure.

Fold centre front seams to inside and insert zip either by hand or machine.

Stitch darts in Hoods. Stitch Hoods together at centre back.

Repeat for lining Hoods. With right sides facing, stitch Hood and Hood lining together around front edge. Turn Hood right side out.

Stitch Hood to neck edge of suit, taking care not to catch lining in seam. Turn under raw edge on lining and slip-stitch over seam.

Fold Front Placket in half lengthwise, right sides together and stitch across short ends.

Turn right side out. Fold in seam allowance on remaining raw edges and baste edges together.

Stitch a 1cm piece of Velcro to inside upper edge of Placket, then top-stitch Placket to right front of suit, as indicated. Stitch corresponding Velcro piece to secure. Stitch imitation fur to front edge of Hood.

Mittens: Finish edges of Mittens with a close, narrow zigzag. (This step isn't necessary if using felt.)

Stitch together in pairs, wrong sides facing, using small handstitches or blanket-stitch.

Cuff can be turned in or out, as desired.

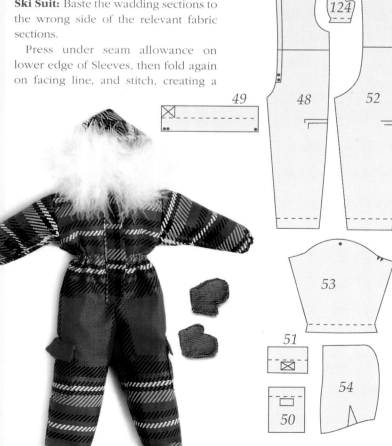

HORSE RIDING OUTFIT

Materials

- Red and black felt
- Scraps of white and beige fabric
- Three tiny buttons in each of red and white
- Six tiny press-studs
- Velcro

Pattern pieces

All pattern pieces are printed on the pattern sheet, Side 1, in black. Trace Jacket Front 55, Jacket Side Front/Back 56, Jacket Back 57, Pocket flap 58, Collar 59, Sleeve 60, Jodhpurs Front 61, Jodhpurs Back 62, Jodhpurs Side Leg Piece 63, Waistband 64, Blouse Front/Back 65 and Necktie 66.

Cutting

Note. Remember to *add* 5mm seam allowance to all pieces, with the following exceptions:

Do not add seam allowance to the Pocket Flaps, the side and outer edges of the Collar, the front and lower edges of the jacket pieces, or the lower edges of the jacket Sleeves.

From red felt, cut two Jacket Fronts, two Jacket Side Front/Backs, one Jacket Back, two Pocket flaps and two Sleeves.

From black felt, cut one Collar.

From beige fabric, cut two Jodhpurs Fronts, two Jodhpurs Backs, two Jodhpurs Side Leg Pieces and one Waistband.

From white fabric, cut one Blouse Front/Back, two Sleeves (pattern piece 60 with added seam allowance) and one Necktie.

Sewing

Jacket: Stitch darts in Jacket Side Front/Backs.

With right sides of felt facing you, place the edges of the side sections beneath the edges of the Fronts and Back so that they just overlap, and top-stitch seams close to edge.

Position Pocket Flaps in position on jacket and top-stitch close to top edge.

With right sides together, stitch Sleeves to armholes, matching side lines.

Stitch shoulder seams, then outside Sleeve seams in one continuous operation.

Place Collar along inner edge of neck and stitch in place close to edge.

Stitch buttons and press-studs in place on front.

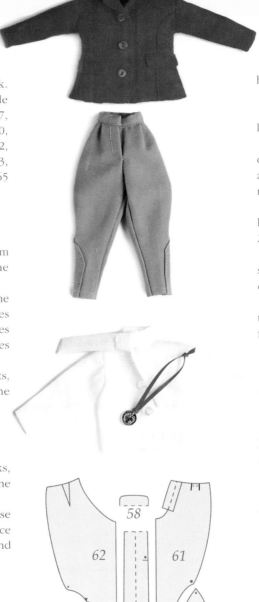

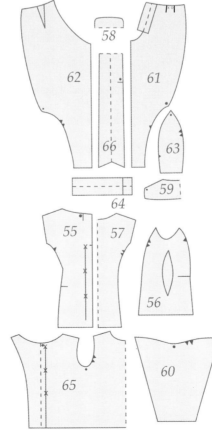

Jodhpurs: Fold pleats in Fronts towards side seams and baste to hold.

Stitch darts in Backs.

Stitch Fronts to Backs at side seams, leaving open below symbol.

Press under seam allowance on curved side edges of Side Leg Pieces and top-stitch in position on Jodhpurs, matching the symbols.

Press under seam allowance on lower edge of Jodhpurs and top-stitch 2mm from edge.

Stitch inside leg seams. Stitch crotch seam from centre back to symbol at centre front.

Fold the fly facing on the right Front to the inside and stitch in place, following given stitching line.

Fold Waistband in half lengthwise, right sides facing, and stitch across ends. Turn right side out.

Stitch one long edge of the Waistband to the Jodhpurs, turn in the seam allowance on remaining long edge and slipstitch it over the seam.

Secure at centre front with a 1cm piece of Velcro.

Blouse: Fold front facing to outside along fold line, stitch along neck edge to centre front, then turn facing back to inside.

Turn in seam allowance on lower edge of Sleeves and top-stitch 2mm from edge.

Gather top of Sleeves slightly and stitch to armholes.

Stitch shoulder seams, then Sleeve seams.

Fold Necktie in half lengthwise, right sides together, and stitch, leaving open between symbols.

Turn right side out. Stitch one edge of Tie to neck edge, matching symbols and centre backs.

Turn in remaining raw edge of Tie and slip-stitch over seam.

Open out front facing at lower edge, top-stitch a narrow hem, then turn the facing back to the inside and catch in place.

Stitch buttons and press-studs in place on the right front.

STRIPED TUNIC TOP, LEGGINGS & SKIRT

(tunic top not photographed)

Materials

- Striped jersey
- Velcro
- Narrow lingerie elastic
- Ric-rac braid

Pattern pieces

All pattern pieces, except the Skirt rectangle, are printed on the pattern sheet, Side 1, in red. Trace Front/Back 67, Neck Binding 68 and Leggings Front/Back 79.

Cutting

Note. Remember to **add** 5mm seam allowance to all pieces.

From striped jersey, cut two

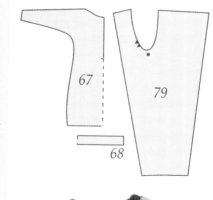

Front/Backs, one Neck Binding, two Leggings Front/Backs, and one Skirt rectangle, 9cm x 34cm (measurements include seam allowance).

Sewing

Tunic Top: Stitch Front to Back at shoulders.

Cut along the split line at the centre back as far as the symbol, and finish the raw edges with a narrow zigzag stitch.

Stitch one long edge of Neck Binding to neck edge.

Fold the Binding in half, right sides together and stitch across the short ends.

Turn Binding right side out again, turn under remaining raw edge and slip-stitch over seam.

Fold lower seam allowance to inside and top-stitch 2mm from edge.

Repeat for lower edge of Sleeves.

Stitch Sleeve and side seams in one continuous operation.

Attach Velcro to neck edge.

Leggings: Press under seam allowance on lower edges and top-stitch 2mm from edge.

Stitch back seams.

Stitch crotch seam from the centre back to centre front.

Apply the elastic to the waist edge, as described under the **General Instructions,** page 76.

Skirt: Stitch centre back seam. Turn up hem on lower edge and top-stitch in place.

Make a narrow casing on the upper edge and thread with elastic to fit waist.

Stitch a row of ric-rac braid around skirt to decorate, if desired.

WAISTCOAT

Materials

- Striped fabric
- Green bias binding
- Three buttons
- Three press-studs

Pattern piece

Pattern piece is printed on the pattern sheet, Side 1, in red. Trace Waistcoat Front/Back 73.

Cutting

Note. Remember to **add** 5mm seam allowance to pattern piece.

From striped fabric, cut one Front/Back.

Sewing

Fold bias binding in half lengthwise and use to bind armholes.

Bind lower edge, then front/neck edge in the same manner.

Stitch shoulder seams, then catch seam allowance in place on inside to prevent bulk.

Attach buttons and press-studs to front opening.

FOLK DRESS

Materials

- Scraps of two different floral prints
- Scrap of checked fabric
- Red bias binding
- Three buttons
- Three press-studs

Pattern pieces

All pattern pieces are printed on the pattern sheet, Side 1, in red. Trace Bodice Front/Back 74, Appliqué Heart 75, Skirt 76, Lower Skirt 77 and Tie 78.

Cutting

Note. Remember to **add** 5mm seam allowance to all pieces.

From one floral print, cut one Bodice Front/Back.

From second print, cut one Skirt and two Ties.

From checked fabric, cut two Appliqué Hearts and one Lower Skirt.

Sewing

Finish edges of Appliqué Hearts with a narrow zigzag stitch and stitch in place on Skirt front, (upper edge can be left unstitched so that Hearts form pockets, if desired).

Stitch Lower Skirt to Skirt, press seam

allowance towards Lower Skirt and top-stitch close to seam. Stitch centre back seam of skirt.

Press under seam allowance on lower edge of skirt and top-stitch 2mm from edge. Run a gathering stitch around upper edge of skirt.

Fold bias binding in half lengthwise, wrong sides facing, and use to bind armhole edges.

Stitch shoulder seams.

Stitch centre back seam of neck facing. Fold facing to outside along given fold line and stitch around neck edge.

Turn facing back to inside, then top-stitch front and neck edges. Lap right front over left front, matching centre fronts, and pin to hold.

Fold Ties in half lengthwise, right sides together, and stitch, leaving one end open. Turn right side out and pin to lower edge of bodice, at each side line.

Pin skirt to bodice, draw up gathers to fit, and stitch, sandwiching Ties at the same time.

Press seam upwards and top-stitch close to seam.

Stitch buttons and press-studs in place on right front.

OVERALLS, SHIRT & BANDANNA

Materials

- Thin denim or chambray
- Checked fabric
- Scrap of gingham
- Four white buttons
- Four tiny jeans buttons
- Five press-studs
- Velcro

Pattern pieces

All pattern pieces are printed on the pattern sheet, Side 1, in red. Trace Overalls Front/Back 80, Overalls Bib 81, Overalls Pocket 82, Strap 83, Back Pocket 84, Shirt Front Facing 85, Shirt Front 86, Shirt Pocket 87, Pocket Flap 88, Shirt Back & Front Yoke 89, Sleeve 90, Collar 91 and Bandanna 72.

Cutting

Note. Remember to **add** 5mm seam allowance to all pieces.

From denim, cut two Overalls Front/Backs, two Bibs, one Overalls Pocket, two Straps and two Back Pockets.

From checked fabric, cut two Shirt Front Facings, two Shirt Fronts, two Shirt Pockets, two Pocket Flaps, one Shirt Back & Front Yoke, two Sleeves and one Collar.

From gingham, cut one Bandanna.

Sewing

Overalls: Fold Back Pocket facings to outside along fold lines and stitch sides. Turn facings back to inside and press under remaining raw edges on Pockets. Top-stitch Pockets in place on back of overalls.

Press under lower edge of overalls on given fold line and top-stitch 1cm from edge, and again, close to first stitching.

Stitch side seams from lower edge to underlap.

Stitch the crotch seam from the centre front to the centre back.

Press under seam allowance on upper, side and underlap edges of back and top-stitch 2mm from edge. Top-stitch along marked stitching lines at upper edge.

Fold front underlaps to inside and top-stitch along given pocket lines and stitching line for fly.

Stitch Bibs together leaving lower edge open. Turn right side out. Stitch outside lower edge of Bib to front of overalls, turn under seam allowance on Bib lining and slip-stitch over seam. Top-stitch Bib around edges and along given stitching lines.

Make Front Pocket in the same way as Back Pockets and top-stitch along top edge.

Place in position on Bib and top-stitch to secure, making two close vertical lines of stitching to divide Pocket in half.

Fold Straps in half lengthwise, right sides facing, and stitch, leaving a small opening for turning. Turn right side out, press and top-stitch around all edges.

Stitch Straps securely to inside back edge of the overalls and finish front ends with a button and press-stud.

Attach 1cm squares of Velcro to underlaps and stitch buttons to waist edge of overalls.

Shirt: Make Pockets as for Overalls and top-stitch to Shirt Fronts.

Stitch Fronts to Back at Yoke seams. Press seam allowance towards Yoke and topstitch close to seam.

Fold Pocket Flaps in half along fold line and stitch, leaving a small opening for turning.

Turn right side out and top-stitch around edges.

Place flaps above Pockets and top-stitch in position.

Stitch Front Facings to front edges of shirt. Fold Facing to outside and stitch along neck edge from fold to centre front.

Turn facings back to inside and top-stitch close to edge.

Fold Collar in half and stitch sides. Turn right side out and stitch one edge to neck edge of shirt. Turn under remaining raw edge and slip-stitch over seam.

Fold under seam allowance on lower edge of Sleeves and top-stitch 2mm from edge. Stitch Sleeves to armholes. Stitch Sleeve and side seams in one continuous operation.

Open out front facings, topstitch a hem on lower edge of shirt, then fold facings back to inside and secure.

Stitch press-studs inside shirt front, then attach buttons on outside right Front.

Bandanna: Work a tiny hem around all edges or hem front edge and fray remaining edges.

JACKET, WRAP SKIRT & HAT

Materials

- Striped woollen fabric
- Scrap of tweed
- Red felt
- Two buttons
- Two press-studs
- Velcro
- Embroidery cotton
- Small gold safety pin

Pattern pieces

All pattern pieces are printed on pattern sheet, Side 1, in red. Trace Jacket Front/Back 92, Pocket 93, Sleeve 94, Skirt Front/Back 95, Waistband 96, Hat Crown 69, Hat Side 70 and Hat Brim 71.

Cutting

Note. Remember to **add** seam allowance to all pieces, except that lower edge of Jacket and Sleeves, outer edge of revers collar (as far as underlap), and outside edge of Hat Brims are all cut without seam allowance, to allow for embroidery.

From woollen fabric, cut one Front/Back, two Pockets and two Sleeves.

From tweed, cut one Skirt Front/Back and one Waistband.

From red felt, cut two Hat Crowns, two Hat Sides and two Hat Brims.

Sewing

Jacket: Fold Pocket facings to inside and work a line of blanket-stitch along top edge. Press under the remaining raw edges on Pockets, then top-stitch in position on front of Jacket.

Finish lower edge of Front/Back and Sleeves with blanket-stitch.

Stitch Sleeves to armholes, matching side lines. Stitch outside Sleeve seams and shoulder seams in one continuous operation, stopping at back neck.

Stitch centre back seam of revers collar, pin collar to neckline and stitch.

Turn under seam allowance on front overlaps and top-stitch 2mm from edge. Finish outer edge of collar as far as underlap with blanket-stitch.

Stitch press-studs inside the jacket opening and stitch the buttons to outside right front.

Wrap Skirt: Fray side edge of overlap for 1cm. Stitch darts.

Turn under seam allowance on lower

edge and top-stitch 5mm from edge.

Fold Waistband in half lengthwise, right sides together and stitch short ends. Turn right side out. Stitch one edge of Waistband to Skirt, turn under remaining raw edge and slip-stitch over seam. Cut a 1cm x 2cm piece of Velcro, align centre fronts of Skirt, then stitch Velcro to overlap and inside of Waistband. Insert small safety pin at centre front, as photographed.

Hat: Stitch short ends of Hat Side together, then stitch Crown in place (this may be easier by hand). Stitch centre back seam of Brim, then stitch Brim to Side (by hand, if necessary). Trim all seams close to stitching. Repeat for second set of hat pieces (lining).

Place hat and lining together, wrong sides facing, and blanket stitch around Brim edges to secure.

BARBIE'S STRIPED KNITS

Measurements

Jumper: The garment measures approximately 7cm; length approximately 7cm; sleeve seam approximately 7cm.
Hat: length approximately 7.5cm.
Leg warmers: Length approximately 11cm.

Materials

Milford Soft Cotton 4-ply (50g):
- Small quantities red, yellow, blue, orange, pink and green
- One pair 3.25mm (No 10) Milward knitting needles
- Three press-studs, for Jumper

Tension: See Knitting and Crochet Notes on page 120. 28 sts to 10cm in width over st st, using 3.25mm needles.

JUMPER

(worked in one piece to armholes)

Using 3.25mm needles and red, cast on 42 sts.

1st row (wrong side). Knit (ridge).

Work 14 rows st st in stripes of 1 row red, 2 rows yellow, 3 rows pink, 1 row green, 2 rows orange, 1 row red, 3 rows blue and 1 row green.

Divide for armholes. Using yellow, K11, *turn* and cont on these sts for Left Back.

Work a further 11 rows, working in stripes of 1 row yellow, 3 rows red, 1 row green, 2 rows orange, 1 row blue, 1 row pink and 2 rows yellow. Cast off.

Join yellow to next 20 sts for Front and, keeping stripes correct as for Left Back for rem, work a further 8 rows st st.

Shape neck. Next row. K8, *turn* and cont on these sts.

Dec at neck edge in every row 3 times. Cast off rem 5 sts.

Join yarn to rem sts, cast off 4 sts, knit to end.

Complete the neck shaping to correspond with other side.

Join yellow to rem 11 sts for Right Back and complete as for Left Back.

Sleeves: Using 3.25mm needles and red, cast on 12 sts.

1st row (wrong side). Knit (ridge). Working in st st and stripe patt as for Jumper, inc at each end of 5th and foll 6th rows 3 times in all...18 sts. Work a further 7 rows. Cast off loosely.

Neck edging: Using back-stitch, join shoulder seams. With right side facing, using 3.25mm needles and red, knit up 22 sts evenly around neck, including back neck.

Cast off loosely knitways.

Right Back Edging: Using 3.25mm needles and red, knit up 19 sts evenly along Right Back edge, including ends of neck and lower edging. Cast off knitways.

Left Back Edging: Work as for Right Back Edging.

To make up

With a slightly damp cloth and warm iron, press lightly. Using back-stitch, join Sleeve seams. Sew in Sleeves. Sew on press-studs, placing one at back neck, one in centre and one at lower edge of Back. Embroider Jumper on Back, Front and Sleeves, as pictured. Press seams.

HAT

Using 3.25mm needles and red, cast on 30 sts.

1st row (wrong side). Knit (ridge). Beg patt. Working throughout in stripe patt as for Jumper, work 8 rows st st.

9th row. K2 tog, *K2, K2 tog, rep from * to end...22 sts.

Work a further 5 rows st st, beg with a purl row.

15th row. K2 tog, *K2 tog, K1, rep from * to last 2 sts, K2 tog...14 sts.

Work a further 5 rows.

21st row. K1, (K2 tog) 6 times, K1...8sts.

Work a further 5 rows.

27th row. (K2 tog) 4 times...4 sts.

Work a further 3 rows. Break off yarn. Thread yarn through rem sts, draw up tightly and fasten off securely.

To make up

With a slightly damp cloth and warm iron, press lightly. Embroider Hat as photographed. Using back-stitch, join centre back seam. Using green, make a small tassel and sew in position to point. Press seams.

LEG WARMERS

(make 2)

Using size 3.25mm needles and red, cast on 14sts.

1st row (wrong side). Knit (ridge). Work 38 rows st st in stripe patt as for Jumper, inc at each end of 7th and foll 8th row...18 sts. Cast off.

To make up

With a slightly damp cloth and warm iron, press lightly. Embroider as photographed. Using back-stitch, join centre back seam. Press seams.

BARBIE'S CABLE KNITS

Measurements

Jumper: The garment measures approximately 8cm; Length approximately 8cm; Sleeve length approximately 7cm. **Scarf:** Width approximately 3cm; length approximately 22cm (excluding the tassels).

Materials

■ One 50g ball 4-ply wool (for set)
■ One pair 3.25mm (No 10) Milward knitting needles
■ Three press-studs, for Jumper

Tension: See Knitting and Crochet Notes page 120.
29 sts to 10cm in width over st st, and 42 sts to 10cm in width over patt, using 3.25mm needles.

Special abbreviations: Twist: Knit into front of second st on lefthand needle (keeping needle in front of first st), then into front of first st, slip both sts off needle tog; TwF: Knit into front of second st on lefthand needle (keeping needle in front of first st), then purl into front of first st, slip both sts off needle tog; TwB: Purl into back of second st on lefthand needle (taking needle behind first st), then knit into front of first st, slip both sts off needle tog.

JUMPER

(worked in one piece to armholes)

Using 3.25mm needles, cast on 66 sts.
1st row (wrong side). Knit (ridge).

Beg patt. 1st row. P1, K1 tbl, *Pl, K1 tbl, P2, Kl tbl, P1, K1 tbl, rep from * to last st, P1.

2nd and alt rows. Knit all knit sts and purl all purl sts as they appear.

3rd row. P1, K1 tbl, *P1, TwB, TwF, P1, K1 tbl, rep from * to last st, P1.

5th row. P1, K1 tbl, *P2, Twist, P2, K1 tbl, rep from * to last st, P1.

7th row. P1, K1 tbl, *P1, TwF, TwB, P1, K1 tbl, rep from * to last st, P1.

8th row. As 2nd row.

Last 8 rows form patt.

Work a further 14 rows patt.

Divide for armholes. Patt 19, *turn* and cont on these sts for Left Back. Keeping patt correct, work a further 11 rows patt. Cast off.

Join yarn to next 28 sts for Front.

Work a further 6 rows patt.

Shape neck. Next row. Patt 11, *turn* and cont on these sts.

Keeping patt correct, dec at neck edge in every row until 6 sts rem. Cast off.

Join yarn to rem sts, cast off next 6 sts, patt to end.

Complete neck shaping to correspond with other side.

Join yarn to rem 19 sts for Right Back and complete as for Left Back.

Sleeves: Using 3.25mm needles, cast on 17sts.

1st row (wrong side). Knit (ridge).

Beg patt. Working in patt as for Front and Backs and noting to work extra sts into patt, inc at each of 3rd and foll 4th rows until there are 27 sts.

Work 5 rows patt. Cast off.

Neckband: Using back-stitch, join shoulder seams.

With right side facing and using 3.25mm needles, knit up 44 sts evenly around neck, incl back neck and overlap.

Knit 3 rows garter st.

Cast off knitways.

To make up

We do not recommend pressing this garment, owing to the textured patt.

Using back-stitch, join Sleeve seams. Sew in Sleeves. Sew press-studs in position, placing one at back neck, one in centre and one at lower edge of Back.

CAP

Using 3.25mm needles, cast on 38sts.

Knit 3 rows garter st (1st row is wrong side).

Work in patt as for Jumper until work measures 4.5cm from beg, working last row on wrong side. Cast off.

To make up

We do not recommend pressing this item, owing to the textured patt. Using back-stitch, join centre back seam. Thread yarn through Cap 5mm below top edge and draw up tightly. Fasten off securely at centre back.

SOCKS

Using 3.25mm needles, cast on 17sts.

Knit 3 rows garter st (1st row is wrong side).

Work 13 rows in patt as for Jumper, **at the same time** dec at each end of 7th row and foll 6th row...13 sts.

Cont in patt until work measures 5cm from beg, working last row on wrong side.

Cast off.

To make up

We do not recommend pressing these items, owing to the textured patt. Using back-stitch, join seam and place to centre back. Join toe seam.

SCARF

Using 3.25mm needles, cast on 8sts.

Work in garter st (every row knit) until work measures 22cm from beg.

Cast off.

To make up

Using 6 strands of yarn, make 8 tassels. Sew 4 tassels in position along each end of Scarf.

PARTY DRESS WITH DETACHABLE SKIRT

Materials

- Pink fabric
- Matching pink satin or silk
- Velcro
- Narrow lingerie elastic

Pattern pieces

All pattern pieces are printed on the pattern sheet, Side 1, in black. Trace Dress Front/Back 101, Side Front/Back Panel 102, Upper Edge Binding 103, Skirt Front/Back 104, Waistband/Tie 105, Detachable Sleeve 106 and Detachable Fitted Shoulder Wrap 107.

Cutting

Note. Remember to **add** 5mm seam allowance to all pieces.

From pink fabric, cut two Dress Front/Backs, cutting one on the fold (without overlap) and the other from double fabric, with overlap. Cut also two Side Front/Back Panels.

From pink silk or satin, cut one Upper Edge Binding, one Skirt Front/Back on the fold, and two Skirt Front/Backs with seam allowance, one Waistband/Tie, two Detachable Sleeves and one Detachable Fitted Shoulder Wrap.

Sewing

Dress: Stitch centre back seam of Backs, leaving open above the underlap symbol. Stitch Side Panels to Front and Back.

Fold under seam allowance on lower edge and top-stitch 2mm from lower edge.

Fold Upper Edge Binding in half lengthwise, right sides together, and stitch sides. Turn right side out. Stitch one edge of Binding to upper edge of Dress, turn under remaining raw edge of Binding and slip-stitch over seam.

Cut a piece of Velcro, 6cm x 1cm, and stitch to left and right underlaps. Fold left underlap to inside and catch in place.

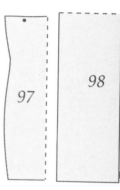

short ends and seam, as far as centre front. Turn Waistband/Ties right side out. Fold the remaining raw edge of the Waistband to inside and slipstitch in place over waist seam.

Detachable Sleeves: Fold under seam allowance on both long edges, then fold under again on fold line and stitch, creating narrow casings. Thread elastic through casings, then stitch side seams, securing elastic ends at the same time.

Detachable Fitted Shoulder Wrap: Fold the Wrap in half lengthwise along the fold line and stitch the long edges together. Turn right side out, and press so that the seamline is in the centre of the strip. Stitch centre front seam.

Gather front edge at centre front and secure gathers with a few hand-stitches.

DISCO DRESS

Materials

- Black ribbed jersey
- Red tulle
- Small red ribbon rose
- 0.5m x 2mm-wide red ribbon

Pattern pieces

All pattern pieces are printed on the pattern sheet, Side 1, in black. Trace Front/Back 97 and Skirt 98.

Cutting

Note. Remember to **add** seam allowance to all pieces.

From ribbed jersey, cut one Front/Back.

From red tulle, cut one skirt.

Sewing

Stitch centre back seam of dress. Fold under seam allowance on upper and lower edges and top-stitch 2mm from edge. Make a small vertical gather at top edge of centre front (to create a

slight décolletage) and stitch ribbon rose in position at this point.

Top-stitch ribbon to lower edge of Skirt. Lap centre back edges narrowly and stitch. Turn under 1cm on upper edge and stitch, forming a narrow casing.

Make a small nick with sharp scissors at centre front of casing and thread remaining ribbon through, pull up to fit lower edge of Skirt and tie ends in a bow.

Hand-stitch Skirt to lower edge of Dress with small stitches

SILK WAISTCOAT & SEQUINNED SKIRT

Materials

- Small amount Thai silk
- 5cm-wide elasticised sequinned band
- Three buttons
- Three press-studs

Pattern pieces

All pattern pieces are printed on the pattern sheet, Side 1, in black. Trace Waistcoat Front/Back 99 and Skirt Front/Back 100.

Cutting

Note. Remember to **add** 5mm seam allowance to all pieces.

From silk, cut two Waistcoat

Skirt: Fold the pleats towards the side seam and baste to hold.

Stitch Fronts to Back at sides. Fold under front and lower edges and top-stitch 2mm from edge.

Stitch one edge of Waistband/Tie to waist edge of Skirt, matching centre backs. Fold Waistband in half length-wise, right sides together, and stitch

GIVE A GIFT SUBSCRIPTION

remembered six times a year
us receive a BONUS PAIR of
WILTSHIRE SCISSORS
th every gift subscription

BONUS WILTSHIRE SCISSORS
with every gift subscription!

Subscribe or send a gift *that lasts all year around*

Yes! Please forward a subscription to **HANDMADE**

☐ Personal   ☐ Gift subscription (please tick one box)
(please tick one box)
☐ 1 year $28.50 (**save $7.20**)
☐ 2 years $57.00 (**save $14.40**)
☐ 1 year New Zealand $A36.70 or $NZ47.70 (*air speeded*)
☐ 1 year overseas $A55.50 (*air speeded*)

FAST PHONE OR FAX
SYDNEY (02) 9260 0012
(8.30am to 5.30pm EST)
ELSEWHERE 1800 25 2515 (*free call*)
Or FAX us on (02) 9267 4363 (*24 hours a day*)

DELIVERY INSTRUCTIONS

Mr/Mrs/Ms _____
          (Initials)   (Surname)

Address _____ Postcode _____

Telephone (work) ( ) _____   (home) ( ) _____

PAYMENT DETAILS

I enclose my cheque/money order for $ _____ payable to **ACP DIRECT**, or charge my:
☐ Bankcard ☐ Visa ☐ MasterCard ☐ American Express ☐ Diners Club

| | | | | | | | | | | | | | | | | |

Exp. Date _____ / _____ Signature _____

HMHL

PAYER DETAILS (*if different from Delivery Details*)

Mr/Mrs/Ms _____
          (Initials)   (Surname)

Address _____ Postcode _____

Telephone (work) ( ) _____   (home) ( ) _____

Yes! Please forward a subscription to **HANDMADE**

☐ Personal   ☐ Gift subscription (please tick one box)
(please tick one box)
☐ 1 year $28.50 (**save $7.20**)
☐ 2 years $57.00 (**save $14.40**)
☐ 1 year New Zealand $A36.70 or $NZ47.70 (*air speeded*)
☐ 1 year overseas $A55.50 (*air speeded*)

FAST PHONE OR FAX
SYDNEY (02) 9260 0012
(8.30am to 5.30pm EST)
ELSEWHERE 1800 25 2515 (*free call*)
Or FAX us on (02) 9267 4363 (*24 hours a day*)

DELIVERY INSTRUCTIONS

Mr/Mrs/Ms _____
          (Initials)   (Surname)

Address _____ Postcode _____

Telephone (work) ( ) _____   (home) ( ) _____

PAYMENT DETAILS

I enclose my cheque/money order for $ _____ payable to **ACP DIRECT**, or charge my:
☐ Bankcard ☐ Visa ☐ MasterCard ☐ American Express ☐ Diners Club

| | | | | | | | | | | | | | | | | |

Exp. Date _____ / _____ Signature _____

HMHL

PAYER DETAILS (*if different from Delivery Details*)

Mr/Mrs/Ms _____
          (Initials)   (Surname)

Address _____ Postcode _____

Telephone (work) ( ) _____   (home) ( ) _____

No postage stamp required
if posted in Australia

REPLY PAID 764
HANDMADE
GPO Box 5252
SYDNEY NSW 1028

No postage stamp required
if posted in Australia

REPLY PAID 764
HANDMADE
GPO Box 5252
SYDNEY NSW 1028

99   100

Front/Backs.

From sequinned band, cut one Skirt front/Back.

Sewing

Waistcoat: Stitch Waistcoats together around all edges except shoulders. Turn right side out through one shoulder and topstitch around finished edges. Stitch shoulder seams together, avoiding lining.

Turn under the raw edges of lining shoulder seams and slip-stitch edges together.

Stitch press-studs in place on inside, then stitch buttons to right front.

Skirt: Stitch centre back seam.

COCKTAIL DRESS

Materials

- Black velvet
- Checked taffeta
- Green tulle
- 0.15m x 2mm-wide red ribbon
- 1m x 1cm-wide black velvet ribbon
- Velcro
- One press-stud

Pattern pieces

All pattern pieces are printed on the pattern sheet, Side 1, in black. Trace Bodice Front 108, Bodice Back 109, Sleeve 110, Front/Back Skirt 111, Bow 112 and Bow Loop 113.

Cutting

Note. Remember to **add** 5mm seam allowance to all pieces.

From black velvet, cut one Front Bodice, two Back Bodices and two Sleeves.

From taffeta, cut two Front/Back Skirts (cutting Front Skirt on the fold, and Back Skirts with centre back seam), one Bow and one Bow Loop.

From tulle, cut two Front/Back Skirts (as for taffeta Skirts).

Sewing

Stitch darts in Front Bodice and Sleeves. Stitch Front to Backs at shoulders.

Fold neckline seam allowance to inside and stitch. Pin red ribbon around neckline and hand-stitch it in place.

Fold under seam allowance on lower edge of Sleeves and top-stitch 2mm from edge. Fold pleats towards sleeve seam and baste to hold. Pin Sleeves to armholes and stitch.

Stitch Sleeve and side seams in one continuous operation.

Fold the left underlap to the inside along centre back line and stitch in place. Fold the seam allowance of right underlap to the inside and top-stitch 2mm from edge. Stitch Velcro to opening to secure.

Stitch centre back seam of Skirt Backs as far as split symbol. Stitch Skirt Front to Back at side seams.

Construct tulle skirt in the same manner as the taffeta skirt.

Position black ribbon along lower edge of tulle skirt and stitch in place close to both edges.

Baste waist edges of both skirts together with small handstitches. Pull up stitches to fit bodice.

Pin bodice to skirt, adjust gathers and stitch.

Fold seam allowance on split to inside and stitch.

Fold Bow in half lengthwise, right sides together, and stitch, leaving a small opening for turning. Turn right side out and slipstitch opening closed. Form bow loops in centre of strip leaving long tails, fold Bow Loop around centre (raw edges folded under) and stitch to hold in bow shape. Stitch completed bow to waist edge of centre back.

Stitch press-stud at waist edge.

113

111   110   109   108

112

Chances are the toy you most cherished, which went with you through childhood into adulthood and perhaps even now sits in a corner of your bedroom, was a teddy bear. Here's a bevy of teddies for you to make as gifts ... if you can bear to give them away.

BEARS TO CHERISH

THE THREE BEARS

Measurements

Papa Bear: Approximately 26cm high.

Mama Bear: Approximately 22cm high.

Baby Bear: Approximately 17cm high.

Materials

Bear pieces are knitted in white yarn, then tea-dyed (instructions follow).

■ For Papa Bear: 2 x 50g balls white 12-ply yarn (we used Cleckheaton Country 12-ply) and one pair of 4mm (No 8) knitting needles

■ For Mama Bear: 2 x 50g balls white 8-ply yarn (we used Cleckheaton Country 8-ply Naturals) and one pair of 3mm (No 11) knitting needles

■ For Baby Bear: 1 x 50g ball white 8-ply yarn (we used Cleckheaton Country 8-ply Naturals) and one pair of 2mm (No 14) knitting needles (Note: We used only two strands of yarn, unravelling one strand as we knitted. If this seems too fiddly, try using 6-ply instead. Size might alter a little.)

■ 0.5m calico, per Bear (optional but recommended)

■ Tea bags for dye mixture

■ Small amount of light brown felt for Paw Pads

■ Five 3cm-diameter plastic joints for Papa Bear

■ Five 3cm-diameter plastic joints for Mama Bear

■ 1cm-diameter safety eyes to use as plastic joints for Baby Bear

■ One pair of 8mm glass safety eyes for Papa Bear;

7mm glass safety eyes for Mama Bear; 5mm glass safety eyes for Baby Bear

■ Craft glue

■ Polyester fibre filling

■ Strong thread (we used linen)

■ Dark brown perle cotton, for Nose

■ Overalls for Papa Bear: 1 x 50g ball white and 1 x 50g ball navy 12-ply yarn; one pair of 5.50mm (No 5) knitting needles; one safety pin

■ Dress for Mama Bear: 1 x 50g ball maroon and 1 x 50g ball white 8-ply yarn; one pair 4mm (No 8) needles

■ Overalls for Baby Bear: 1 x 50g ball green and 1 x 50g ball white 8-ply or 6-ply yarn (we used two strands only unravelling one strand during knitting); one pair of 3mm (No 11) knitting needles; one safety pin

■ Two matching buttons for each piece of Bear's clothing (omit if making for younger children)

BEARS

Using appropriate yarn and needles, work Head pieces, Gusset, Ear pieces, Arm pieces, Body pieces and Leg pieces from Graphs (yarn and needle size dictate size of Bear). Pieces are worked in rev st st (beg by purling sts on 1st row of each Graph) so purl fabric is right side of work.

Dyeing and felting pieces

Do not dye all pieces for all three Bears together (best results are achieved by dyeing all Papa Bear pieces, then using a new mixture to dye Mama Bear pieces, and another new mixture to dye Baby Bear pieces).

Boil 2 litres of water with 10 teacup-sized teabags. Add Bear pieces (and felt Paw pieces, if desired) and simmer for 15 minutes. Using tongs, remove pieces from tea mixture and place under cold running water for about 5 minutes (until yarn cools down). Return pieces to tea mixture and simmer for a further 5 minutes. Using tongs, rinse under running water again. Wrap pieces in a towel and squeeze out water. While pieces are wet, comb or brush right side of pieces (purl side) for a felted effect (the steel side of a pet brush works well). Leave pieces to dry on a flat surface.

To make up

From felt, and using pattern outlines given, cut two Paw Pads and two Foot Pads, per Bear, in appropriate size. When knitted pieces are dry, place them onto calico and, allowing

THREE BEARS

This is the story of the three bears. They're all knitted from the same pattern – Papa Bear in 12 ply, Mama Bear in 8 ply and Baby Bear in 6 ply. But the real secret to their soft, fuzzy, cuddly charm, is that they are tea-dyed then felted with a stiff wire brush before the pieces are joined together.

HEAD

Work one of each piece

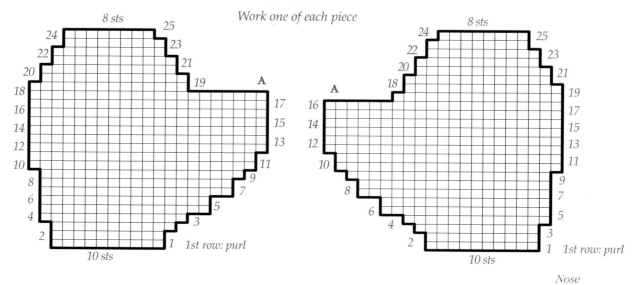

8 sts   25

24
22
20
19   A
18
16   17
14   15
12   13
10   11
8   9
6   7
4   5
2   3
1   1st row: purl
10 sts

24   8 sts   25
22   23
20   21
A   18   19
16   17
14   15
12   13
10   11
8   9
6   7
4   5
2   3
1   1st row: purl
10 sts

ARMS

Work one of each full Arm. Work one of each without Paws
(Four pieces in all)

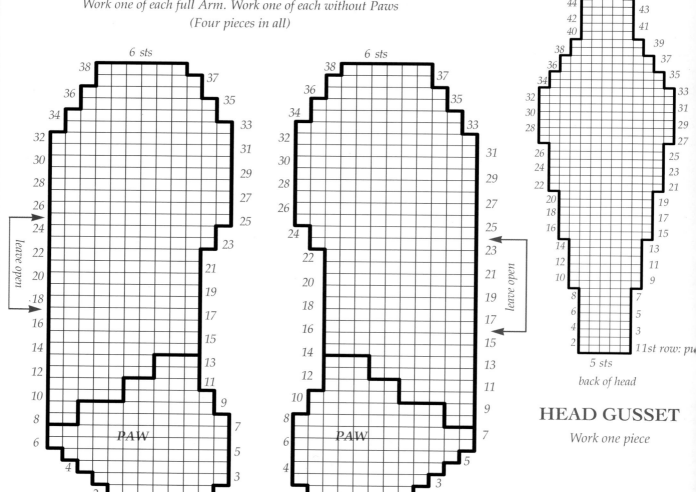

6 sts

38   37
36   35
34   33
32   31
30   29
28   27
26   25
24   23
leave open   22   21
20   19
18   17
16   15
14   13
12   11
10   9
8   PAW   7
6   5
4   3
2   1   1st row: purl
5 sts

6 sts
38   37
36   35
34   33
32   31
30   29
28   27
26   25
24   23   leave open
22   21
20   19
18   17
16   15
14   13
12   11
10   9
8   PAW   7
6   5
4   3
2   1   1st row: purl
5 sts

Nose
A   47
46   45
44   43
42   41
40   39
38   37
36   35
34   33
32   31
30   29
28   27
26   25
24   23
22   21
20   19
18   17
16   15
14   13
12   11
10   9
8   7
6   5
4   3
2   11st row: pu
5 sts
back of head

HEAD GUSSET

Work one piece

BODY

Work two pieces

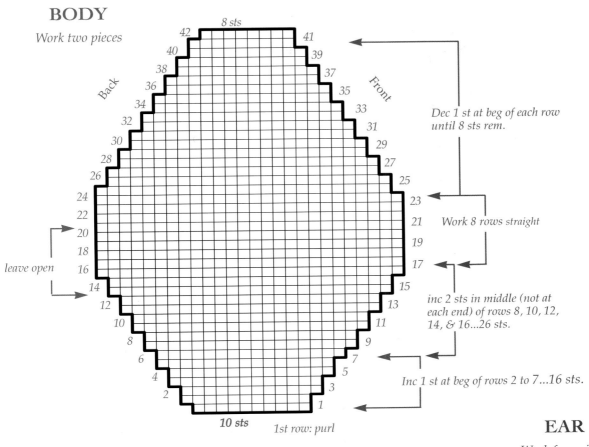

8 sts

42 41
40   39
38   37
Back 36   35 Front
34   33
32   31
30   29
28   27
26   25

24   23

Dec 1 st at beg of each row until 8 sts rem.

22   21
20   *leave open* 19

18   17

Work 8 rows straight

16   15

inc 2 sts in middle (not at each end) of rows 8, 10, 12, 14, & 16...26 sts.

14   13
12   11
10   9
8   7
6   5
4   3
2   1

10 sts   *1st row: purl*

Inc 1 st at beg of rows 2 to 7...16 sts.

EAR

Work four pieces

5 sts

8   7
6   5
4   3
2   1

1st row: purl

LEGS

Work four of each (four pieces in total)

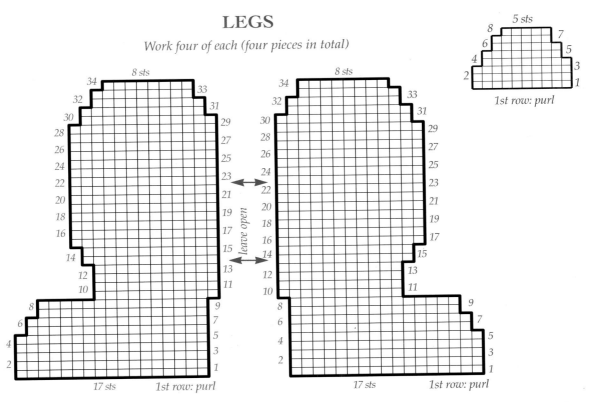

8 sts   8 sts

34   33   34   33
32   31   32   31
30   29   30   29
28   27   28   27
26   25   26   25
24   23 ↔ 22 24   23
22   21   *leave open* 21
20   19   20   19
18   17   18   17
16   15 ↔ 14 16   15
14   13   14   13
12   11   12   11
10   9   10   9
8   7   8   7
6   5   6   5
4   3   4   3
2   1   2   1

17 sts   *1st row: purl*   17 sts   *1st row: purl*

a small seam allowance, cut out each piece (except Ears) in calico. This is particularly important for the Head, as it prevents the bear's Head from being stretched out of shape while stuffing. We also recommend it for the other body parts, but it can be omitted if you wish. If making a calico body, don't forget Foot Pad sections (although you don't need Paw Pads; simply cut two pairs of Outer Arms).

With right sides together, stitch Head pieces to each side of Head Gusset, matching point A on nose. Turn right side out. Construct calico Head in the same way, insert calico Head into wool Head (with wrong side of wool facing right side of calico, so that calico seams won't be visible). Run a strong gathering thread around neck edge, through both layers.

With right sides together, join Body pieces, leaving an opening at centre back for filling. Turn right side out. Construct calico Body in the same way. Place calico Body inside wool Body (as for Head), and run a strong gathering thread around neck edge. With right sides facing, join Leg sections together in pairs, leaving an opening in back seam for filling. With right sides together, stitch Foot Pad in place at lower end of each Leg. Turn right side out. Construct and insert calico Legs.

With right sides together, stitch Paw Pad to Inner Arm, then, with right sides together, stitch Inner Arm to Outer Arm in pairs, leaving an opening in back seam for filling. Turn right side out. Construct and insert calico Arms.

Attach safety eyes to Head, then stuff Head with polyester filling. With right sides facing, stitch Ears together in pairs, leaving straight edge open. Turn right side out.

With a strong thread and avoiding stitches showing, take a stitch through Bear's snout, from eye straight down to chin, then back up to second eye and down to chin again, pulling thread slightly, to create eye sockets and to accentuate snout a little. Tie off thread securely under the chin and bury ends. Place plastic joint pieces into Head and Body, pull up gathers around joints and fasten off, then snap joint together, thus connecting Head to Body.

Join Arms and Legs to Body using plastic joints. Stuff limbs and Body with polyester filling and stitch openings closed, stitching the calico and wool separately.

Stitch Ears in place on Head.

For nose, cut a small triangular shape from felt, glue it in position, then cover it completely with straight-stitches, using brown perle thread, extending stitching below nose for mouth, as photographed. (The felt nose can be omitted but it gives the embroidered nose more substance.)

PAPA BEAR'S OVERALLS

Back

First Leg. Using 5.50mm needles and white yarn, cast on 12 sts.

1st row. *K1, P1; rep from * to end. Rep last row once more. Cont in st st stripes of 2 rows navy and 2 rows white, work 6 rows.** Dec one st at beg of next and foll alt row...10 sts. Work one row. Leave sts on a safety pin.

Second leg. Work as for First Leg to **. Dec one st at end of next and foll alt row...10 sts.

Work one row.

Join Legs. Next row. Using white

yarn, K10 Second Leg sts, then knit across right-side of First Leg sts from safety pin...20 sts.

Keeping stripes correct, work a further 15 rows, beg with a purl row.

Shape for waist. Cont in st st stripes, cast off 2 sts at beg of next 2 rows...16 sts. Work a further 6 rows in st st stripes.***

Cont in white garter st for rem, work 10 rows.

Shape Back neck. Next row. K4, *turn.* Cont on these 4 sts only, knit one row.

Next row. K2tog, K1. Cast off.

With right side facing, join yarn to rem 12 sts, cast off next 8 sts, knit to end...4 sts.

Next row. Knit.

Next row. K2tog, K1. Cast off.

Front

Work as for Back to ***.

Cont in white garter st for rem, work 4 rows.

Shape Front neck. Next row. K7, *turn.* Cont on these 7 sts, dec one st at end of alt rows 4 times...3 sts. Cast off.

With right side facing, join yarn to rem 9 sts, cast off next 2 sts, knit to end. Cont on these 7 sts, dec one st at beg of alt rows 4 times...3 sts. Cast off.

To make up

Join Side seams to waist. Join inside Leg seams. Join shoulder seams, or crochet buttonloops to the Front shoulders. Stitch buttons to shoulders, if desired.

MAMA BEAR'S DRESS

Back

Using white yarn and 4mm needles, cast on 32 sts.

1st row. *K1, P1; rep from * to end. Rep last row once more.

Cont in st st stripes of 2 rows maroon and 2 rows white, work 22 rows st st.

23rd row. Using white, knit.

Shape waist. 24th row. Using white, (K2tog) to end...16 sts.****

Cont in white garter st for rem, work 14 rows.

Shape Back neck. Complete as for Back of Papa Bear's Overalls.

Front

Work as for Back to ****.

Cont in white garter st for rem, work 8 rows.

Shape Front neck. Complete as for Front of Papa Bear's Overalls.

To make up

Join side seams to waist. Join the shoulder seams, or crochet button-loops to Front shoulders. Stitch buttons to shoulders, if desired.

BABY BEAR'S OVERALLS

Note. Use only 2 stands of each coloured 8-ply yarn (unravel one strand as you go, or use 6-ply).

Back

Work as for Back of Papa Bear's Overalls, noting the foll exceptions. Use 3mm needles, and 2 strands of green yarn in place of navy.

Work 11 rows (not 15) before waist shaping.

Work 2 rows (not 6) in st st stripes before starting garter st.

Front

Work as for Front of Papa Bear's Overalls, noting to work 11 rows (not 15) before waist shaping and 2 rows (not 6) in st st stripes before starting garter st.

To make up

Make up as for Papa Bear's Overalls, above.

A: Papa Bear Foot
B: Baby Bear Foot
C: Baby Bear Paw
D: Mama Bear Foot
E: Papa Bear Paw
F: Mama Bear Paw

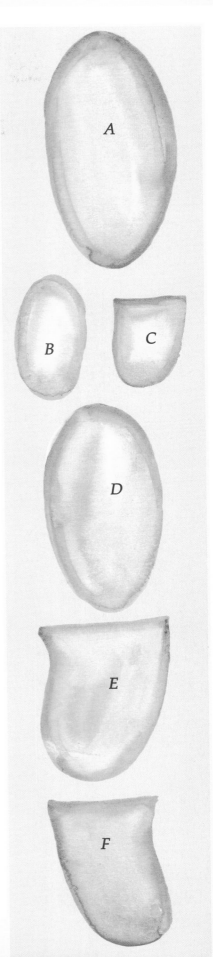

TWO VERY SUPERIOR BEARS

Measurements

Finished bear is approximately 34cm tall.

Materials

- 50cm x 70cm fur fabric
- Fray-Check
- One set of joints (Size 4A): 4x 30mm wooden discs for arms, 6 x 40mm wooden discs for neck and legs, 5 screws and lock nuts, 10 small washers
- Felt for joints (optional)
- One pair 12mm glass or safety eyes
- Doll needle
- 16cm square felt or suede, for paws
- Brown Coton Perle 8 for nose
- Strong thread or waxed dental floss
- Machine thread to match fabric
- Polyester filling

Note. Fur fabrics, joints and eyes are all available from teddy bear and doll specialists. See page 120 for mail order suppliers.

Oscar and Lucinda are made in a distressed synthetic fabric which has a knitted back. Because of the stretch, knitback fur fabrics cannot be stuffed as firmly as woven-backed fabrics and thus the finished bear is more cuddly than traditional or character bears.

If the bear is to be made for a toddler, glass eyes are **not** suitable. Use plexi safety lock eyes instead.

Pattern pieces

All pattern pieces are printed on pattern sheet, Side 4, in pink tone. Trace Side Head, Head Gusset, Ear, Body, Arm, Leg, Paw Pad, Foot Pad.

Cutting

Note. 3.5mm seam allowance is **included** on all pieces. Stick traced pattern pieces onto thin card or template plastic and carefully cut out pieces to make templates. Position the templates as shown in layout diagram and draw around them using a fine line marker or pencil. Take care to reverse pattern pieces when required (as shown in layout diagram) and ensure that pile of fabric runs in the direction shown by grain lines on pattern pieces. Always use small sharp pointed scissors and cut very carefully, running scissors under the pile and cutting the backing only.

From fur fabric, cut two Side Heads, one

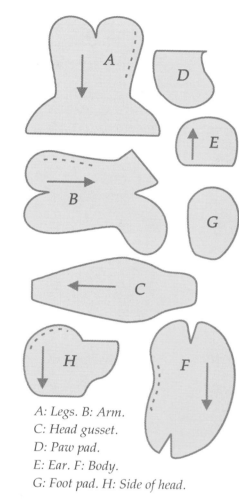

A: Legs. B: Arm.
C: Head gusset.
D: Paw pad.
E: Ear. F: Body.
G: Foot pad. H: Side of head.

Head Gusset, four Ears, two Bodies, two Arms and two Legs.

From felt or suede, cut two Paw Pads and two Foot Pads.

Sewing

Apply Fray-Check sparingly to the very edge of cut edges of fur fabric to prevent fraying and stretching. Avoid applying it to the seamline. If fabric is very soft and has a tendency to fray, then apply Fray-Check to all cut edges before sewing. Firm-backed fabrics only need to be treated where seams are left open for turning.

Unless otherwise specified, all seams are stitched with right sides together.

OSCAR AND LUCINDA

No nursery is complete without a thoroughly superior bear, and Oscar and Lucinda both fit the bill. You can also make their smart outfits.

Joining head to body.

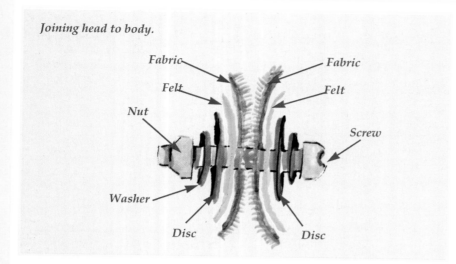

Fabric · Fabric · Felt · Felt · Nut · Screw · Washer · Disc · Disc

Pin and stitch Side Head centre front seam joining A to B under chin. Pin and stitch Head Gusset to Sides joining A to C, leaving an opening where indicated, on one side only. With strong thread and by hand, run a gathering thread around neck edge. Draw up and secure off tightly. Turn right side out and, if using safety lock eyes, make a small hole with pointed scissors at positions marked on pattern and insert eyes.

Matching Es and Ds on Paw Pad and Arm, pin and sew paws to inner arm. Fold arm in half, right side of fabric facing. Pin and sew around top of arm and down around paw leaving the opening from F to G, as marked. Turn to right side. Repeat for second arm.

Match Ears in pairs, pin and sew around curve. Turn right side out. Turn raw edge up 3.5mm and, by hand, over-sew the two pieces together across the base. Leave to fix later.

Fold Leg in half, right sides of fabric together, pin and sew H to I and J to K, leaving opening as indicated. Pin Foot Pad in place by matching Pad centre L to centre seam of leg and easing foot pad around evenly. Stitch. Turn right side out. Repeat for second leg.

Pin and sew the darts in Body as indicated and sew two body pieces, leaving a 3.5mm opening at neck where darts meet. Also leave opening at back of body between M and N, as indicated. Turn to right side.

To join head to body, place washer, then disc onto screw, followed by a circle of felt a little larger than the disc and with hole made in the centre. (Felt is optional and used to avoid friction of disc against the fabric.) Screw is then placed into the head through top opening and the shaft pushed through gathering at base of neck to protrude out of head. Protruding screw is then pushed through hole at neck on top of body. Place another piece of felt on screw protruding into body followed by disc and washer then lock nut (see diagram above).

Finger-tighten lock nut onto end of screw then continue to tighten until secure and snug by using a ring spanner on lock nut and turning screw head with a screwdriver.

Make holes with pointed scissors at joint marks on the Arms and Legs and on the Body. To attach arms and legs, follow the same steps for attaching

head, making sure that the joint construction is quite firm to turn or legs and arms will flop.

Stuffing and finishing

Use coarse thread or dental floss to close all seams, using ladder stitch as follows: Using strong thread, pick up a few threads of fabric along the seamline on one side, then pick up the same distance along the other side of the opening. The crossover thread represents a rung of the ladder, and the pick-up sections represent the side supports (see diagram below left).

Arms and legs: Stuff arms and legs firmly, making sure that filling is pushed well down into paws. Ladder stitch openings to close. With perle thread, embroider claws at toes and paws, taking tiny back stitches to secure thread.

Head: Stuff head firmly, moulding into shape as you go. The personality of the bear can be changed by this moulding and shaping. Close opening on top of head with ladder stitch. Using perle thread, embroider nose and mouth as desired (see diagram below). Begin by putting a knot in the centre of area to be covered. Experiment, keeping stitches close together and going over and over to build up snout. When finished, run the needle back under your stitches, catching the material, and then back again to secure the thread.

Pin ears into preferred position and ladder stitch in place at back. The position of the eyes and ears can change the look of the bear immensely, so take care with placement.

Body: Stuff body firmly, making sure plenty of stuffing is pushed around neck

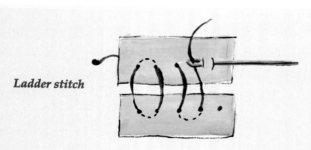

Ladder stitch

Nose styles

and arm joints and down around leg joints. Ladder stitch opening to close.

Eyes: If using glass eyes, determine the position of the eyes and make a very small hole in that position. Thread a long piece of coarse thread through the loop at the back of the eye and then thread the two ends together onto a long needle. Pass the needle into the head through the eye position and out the back of the head at the base of the neck. Repeat with other eye, coming out as close as possible to first string. Pull eyes firmly down into head to create a small depression and tie a reef knot to secure all ends. Re-thread all ends on needle and bury ends back in centre of head. The wire hook on back of glass eye should slip down into the hole and not sit up outside the fabric. Use a wire or coarse brush to fluff up teddy all over.

TEDDY'S WARDROBE

Measurements

To fit a teddy approximately 36cm tall. Chest: 32cm; waist: 33cm; hips (around top of legs): 38cm.

Materials

SHIRT
- 0.3 m x 115cm fabric
- Three x 1cm-diameter buttons
- Three small press-studs

TROUSERS
- 0.3mx 115cm fabric
- Two x 1cm-diameter buttons
- Four small press-studs

SKIRT
- 0.3m x 115cm fabric
- Two x 1cm-diameter buttons
- Four small press-studs

KNICKERS
- 0.25m x 115cm fabric
- 0.5m x 3mm-wide elastic

BOW TIE
- Small scrap of fabric
- 0.2m x 6mm-wide elastic
- One medium press-stud

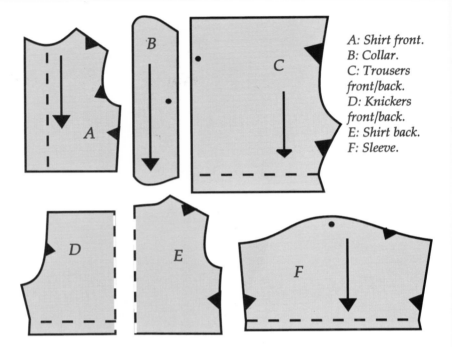

A: Shirt front.
B: Collar.
C: Trousers front/back.
D: Knickers front/back.
E: Shirt back.
F: Sleeve.

Pattern pieces

All pattern pieces, except rectangles, are printed on pattern sheet, Side 4, in black. Trace Shirt Front, Shirt Back, Collar, Sleeve, Trousers Front/Back and Knickers Front/Back.

Cutting

Note. 5mm seam allowance is included on all pattern pieces and measurements, unless otherwise specified.

From Shirt fabric, cut two Shirt Fronts, one Shirt Back, two Collars and two Sleeves.

From Trousers fabric, cut four Front/Backs, two rectangles, each 22cm x 7cm, for Waistbands, and two rectangles, each 24cm x 7cm, for Straps.

From Skirt fabric, cut two rectangles, each 40cm x 15cm, for Skirts, two rectangles, each 70cm x 10cm, for Frill, two rectangles, each 22cm x 7cm, for Waistbands, and two rectangles, each 24cm x 7cm, for Straps.

From Knickers fabric, cut two Front/Backs.

Sewing

SHIRT

With right sides together, stitch Fronts to Back at the shoulder seams. Press seams open.

Press under hem allowance on lower edges of Sleeves, turn under raw edge and top-stitch in place. Run a row of ease-stitching around top of Sleeves, between notches. With right sides together, fit Sleeve to armhole, pull up ease-stitching to fit, distributing fullness evenly, then stitch. Neaten seam.

With right sides together, stitch side and Sleeve seams in one continuous operation, matching underarm seams, and hem edges.

With right sides together, stitch Collars together, leaving neck edge open. Clip curves, turn Collar right side out and press. Baste raw edges together. With right sides together and raw edges even, baste Collar to neck edge of Shirt, matching centre backs.

Press under 5mm on raw opening edges of Fronts. Turn front facing to outside on fold line, right sides together, sandwiching Collar at the same time. Stitch along neck edge. Use zigzag or overlocking to neaten raw edges of seam. Turn front facing back to inside and press.

Top-stitch or hand-sew a narrow hem on lower edge.

Sew three evenly spaced buttons to right or left Front (left Front for boy, or right Front for girl), then lap buttoned Front over remaining side and sew three small press-studs beneath buttons to secure front opening.

TROUSERS

With right sides facing, join Trouser sections together in pairs along the centre front/back crotch seam.

With right sides together, stitch Front to Back at side seams, leaving open above small dots. Press seam open, including seam allowance above small dot, then top-stitch around opening edges to neaten, squaring stitching across seam at small dot.

With right sides together, stitch inside leg seam, matching crotch seams. Machine- or hand-finish hems on lower edges.

Run a gathering thread along waist edge of Front and Back. Draw up gathers to fit Waistbands, leaving 5mm extending on each end of Waistband. With right sides together and raw edges even, stitch a Waistband to Front and Back. Press under 5mm on remaining long raw edge of each Waistband.

With right sides together, fold Waistbands in half lengthwise and stitch short ends. Fold Waistband back to inside and slip-stitch pressed edge in place over seam. Press.

With right sides together, fold each Strap in half lengthwise and stitch along long edge and one short edge. Turn Straps right side out and press.

Position raw edges of Straps behind front Waistband so that they are evenly spaced on either side of centre front. Top-stitch close to all edges of front and back Waistbands, catching Straps in position at the same time.

Stitch a button to each end of front Waistband. Try Trousers on teddy. Lap ends of front Waistband over back Waistband to fit and sew press studs beneath buttons to secure.

Adjust length of Straps to fit and secure in place on inside back Waistband with press-studs.

SKIRT

With right sides facing, join Skirt rectangles together at sides, leaving 6cm open on upper edge of each seam. Press seams open, including seam allowance on opening edges, then topstitch around opening edges to neaten, squaring stitching across lower edge of opening.

Frill: With right sides facing, join Frill rectangles together at short edges, forming a large circle. Press seams open, then press Frill in half lengthwise, wrong sides together. Run a gathering thread around raw edges of Frill and draw up to fit lower edge of Skirt.

With right sides together, raw edges even, and matching side seams, pin Frill to lower edge of Skirt.

Adjust gathers to fit, then stitch. Trim and neaten seam, then press seam allowance towards Skirt.

Waistband, straps and finishing: Finish Waistbands and Straps as for Trousers, left.

KNICKERS

Press under 3cm on leg edge of each Knicker piece. Cut two pieces of elastic to fit around teddy's leg and, with elastic placed over turned in raw edge, stitch elastic to Knickers using a narrow zigzag, stretching elastic gently to fit as you sew. With right sides together, stitch inside leg seams, stitching across elastic ends at the same time. Neaten seam with zigzag or overlocking. With right sides together, stitch crotch seam from centre front to centre back, matching inside leg seams. Neaten seam.

Press under 5mm on upper raw edge, then turn under another 1cm and stitch to form casing, leaving opening at centre back to thread elastic. Cut a piece of elastic to fit teddy's waist, thread through casing, adjust to fit, secure ends, then stitch opening closed.

BOW TIE

Cut a scrap of fabric, 14cm x 5cm, and finger press in half crosswise to mark centre point. Bringing right sides together, fold each end back towards centre point so that they just meet, forming a rectangle, 7cm x 5cm. Stitch along top and bottom edges, turn right side out through centre back opening and press.

Cut another piece of the same fabric, 3cm x 5cm. Press under 5mm on each longer edge.

Wrap this shorter piece around the centre of the Tie rectangle, pulling it up to give a bow tie effect. Secure raw ends at back.

Stitch Bow Tie onto one end of elastic and stitch press-stud to ends of the elastic.

Secure around teddy's neck.

JUMPER WITH STRIPES

Measurements

Fits chest: 36cm. Length: approximately 16cm. Sleeve seam: 10cm.

Materials

8-ply yarn (100g):
■ One ball each of 3 colours (Cl: yellow, C2: red, C3: purple)
■ One pair each 4mm (No 8) and 3mm (No 11) knitting needles
■ Three stitch-holders
■ Three buttons

Tension: See **Knitting and Crochet Notes**, page 120.
22.5 sts and 29.5 rows to 10cm over st st, using 4mm needles.

Back

Using C1 and 3mm needles, cast on 43 sts.
Knit 5 rows garter st (1st row is wrong side).
Change to 4mm needles.
Work 10 rows st st.
Using C2, work 14 rows st st.**
Divide for Back opening. 1st row. K24, *turn* and cont on these 24 sts.
2nd row. K5, purl to end.
Change to C3 for rem.
3rd row. Knit.

4th row. As 2nd row.
5th row. Knit to last 3 sts, yfwd, K2tog, K1 . ..buttonhole.
Rep 2nd and 3rd rows 3 times, then 2nd row once.
13th row. As 5th row.
Rep 2nd and 3rd rows twice, then 2nd row once.
Cast off 11 sts at beg of next row, knit to end.
20th row. K5, purl to end.
Leave rem 13 sts on a stitchholder.
With right side facing, join C2 to rem 19 sts, cast on 5 sts for underlap, knit to end...24 sts.
2nd row. Purl to last 5 sts, K5.
Change to C3 for rem.
3rd row. Knit.
Rep 2nd and 3rd rows 8 times
Cast off 11 sts at beg of next row, purl to last 5 sts, K5.
Leave rem 13 sts on a stitchholder.

Front

Work as for Back to **.
Using C2, work 2 rows st st.
Using C3 for rem, work 6 rows st st.
Shape neck. Next row. K17, *turn* and cont on these 17 sts.
***Dec one st at neck edge in every row until 11 sts rem.
Work 3 rows.
Cast off.***
With right side facing, slip next 9 sts on a stitch-holder and leave. Join C3 to rem 17 sts and knit to end.
Work as from *** to ***, noting to work 4 rows instead of 3 before casting off.

Sleeves

Using C2 and 3mm needles, cast on 37 sts.
Knit 5 rows garter st (1st row is wrong side).
Change to 4mm needles.

Work 10 rows st st, inc one st at each end of 5th row...39 sts.
Using C3 for rem, inc one st at each end of next and foll 6th row...43sts.
Work 7 rows. Cast off loosely.

Neckband

Using back-stitch, join the shoulder seams. With right side facing, using C3 and 3mm needles, knit across sts from left Back stitch-holder, knit up 10 sts evenly along left side of neck, knit across sts from Front stitch-holder, knit up 10 sts evenly along right side of neck, then knit across sts from right Back stitch-holder...55 sts.
Knit 5 rows garter st, working a buttonhole (as before) at end of 2nd row...3 buttonholes altogether.
Cast off knitways.

To make up

Do not press. Tie coloured threads 9cm down from the shoulders on side edges of Back and Front to mark armholes. Using back-stitch, sew in Sleeves evenly between coloured threads, placing centre of Sleeves to shoulder seams. Join side and Sleeve seams. Sew underlap in position. Sew on buttons.

CARDIGAN WITH EMBROIDERED HEARTS

Measurements

Fits chest: 36cm. Length: approximately 16cm. Sleeve seam: 10cm.

Materials

8-ply yarn (100g):
■ Main Colour (MC, blue): 1 ball
■ Contrast Colours (red, yellow, purple): small quantity of each
■ One pair each 4mm (No 8) and 3mm (No 11) knitting needles
■ Two buttons
■ Tapestry needle for sewing seams and embroidery

Tension: See **Knitting and Crochet Notes** page 120.

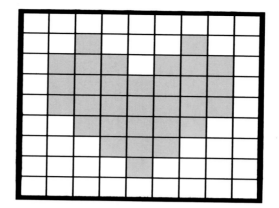

22.5 sts and 29.5 rows to 10cm over st st, using 4mm needles.

Back

Using MC and 3mm needles, cast on 43 sts.
1st row. K2, *P1, K1; rep from * to last st, K1.
2nd row. K1 *P1, K1; rep from * to end.
Rep 1st and 2nd rows 3 times...8 rows rib in all.
Change to 4mm needles. Cont in st st until work measures 7cm from beg, ending with a purl row.
Tie a coloured thread at each end of last row to mark beg of armholes as there is no armhole shaping.
Work 26 rows st st.
Cast off 12 sts at beg of next 2 rows.
Cast off rem 19 sts.

Left Front

Using MC and 3mm needles, cast on 21 sts.
Work 8 rows rib as for Back. Change to 4mm needles.
Cont in st st until the work measures same as Back to armhole, ending with a purl row.**
Tie a coloured thread at the end of the last row to mark beg of the armhole.
Shape front slope. Cont in st st, dec one st at end (front edge) of next and foll alt rows until 14 sts rem, then in foll 4th rows until 12 sts rem.
Work 5 rows.
Cast off.

Right Front

Work as for Left Front to **.
Tie a coloured thread at beg of last row to mark beg of the armhole.

Shape front slope. Cont in st st, dec one st at beg (front edge) of next and foll alt rows until 14 sts rem, then in foll 4th rows until 12 sts rem.
Work 6 rows.
Cast off.

Sleeves

Using MC and 3mm needles, cast on 35 sts.
Work 8 rows rib as for Back.
Change to 4mm needles.
Cont in st st, inc one st at each end of 3rd and foll 6th rows until there are 43 sts.
Cont straight in st st until work measures 10cm from beg, ending with a purl row.
Cast off loosely.

Right Front Band

Using back-stitch, join the shoulder seams. With right side facing, using MC and 3mm needles, knit up 16 sts evenly along Front edge to beg of front slope shaping, 26 sts evenly along front slope to shoulder, then 9 sts evenly across half of Back neck...51sts.
Work 3 rows rib as for Back, beg with a 2nd row.
4th row. Rib 4, yfwd, K2tog, rib 8, yfwd, K2tog, rib to end...2 buttonholes.
Work 3 rows rib.
Cast off loosely in rib.

Left Front Band

Work to correspond with Right Front Band, omitting buttonholes and beg at centre Back neck.

To make up

Do not press. Using knitting-stitch (see page 36) and Contrast Colours, embroider the heart motif from the Graph, above, to Back, Fronts and Sleeves at random.
Using back stitch, sew in the Sleeves evenly between the coloured threads, placing the centre of Sleeves to the shoulder seams.
Join side and Sleeve seams.
Sew on buttons.

SMALL
ONE

*Just a handful of sheer
delight, Scallywag is the
ultimate collector's bear.*

SCALLYWAG

Measurements

Bear is 25cm tall (18cm sitting).

Materials

- 50cm x 35cm Mohair or synthetic fur fabric, pile length 5mm
- Fray-Check
- One set of joints (Size 2): 25mm discs for head, 20mm for limbs (see **Note**)
- One pair 7mm or 8mm glass eyes
- Doll needle
- 7.5cm square felt or suede, for paws
- Brown Coton Perle 8 or stranded cotton, for nose
- Strong thread, for sewing
- Small bag polyester filling and/or pellets
- Ribbon for neck bow, optional

Note. Fur fabrics, joints and eyes are all available from teddy bear and doll specialists.

Pattern pieces

All pattern pieces are printed on pattern sheet No 4 in red. Trace Side Head A, Head Gusset B, Muzzle C, Ear D, Side Front F, Side Back I, Outer Arm H, Inner Arm K, Paw Pad J, Leg E and Foot Pad G.

Note. 3.5mm seam allowance is included on all pieces. Stick traced pattern pieces onto thin card or template plastic and carefully cut out pieces to make templates. Position the templates as shown in layout diagram, and draw around them using a fine line marker or pencil. Take care to reverse pattern pieces when required (as shown in layout diagram) and ensure that pile of fabric runs in the direction shown by grain lines on pattern pieces. Always use small sharp pointed scissors and cut carefully, running the scissors under the pile and cutting the backing only.

From fur fabric, cut two Side Heads, one Head Gusset, one Muzzle, four Ears, two Side Fronts, two Side Backs, two Outer Arms, two Inner Arms and four Legs.

From felt or suede, cut two Paw Pads (reversing pattern piece for second pad) and two Foot Pads.

Sewing

Apply Fray-Check sparingly to the very edge of cut edges of fur fabric, to prevent fraying and stretching. Avoid applying it to the seamline. If fabric is very soft and has a tendency to fray, then apply Fray-Check to all cut edges before sewing. Firm-backed fabrics only need to be treated where seams are left open for turning.

Before seaming, pieces should be carefully oversewn together, by hand. As you work, use the needle to push the fur pile down between the two pieces to ensure well-covered seams. The final seaming can be done by hand, using neat small back-stitch and strong thread, or by machine, stitching carefully along the seamline. Unless

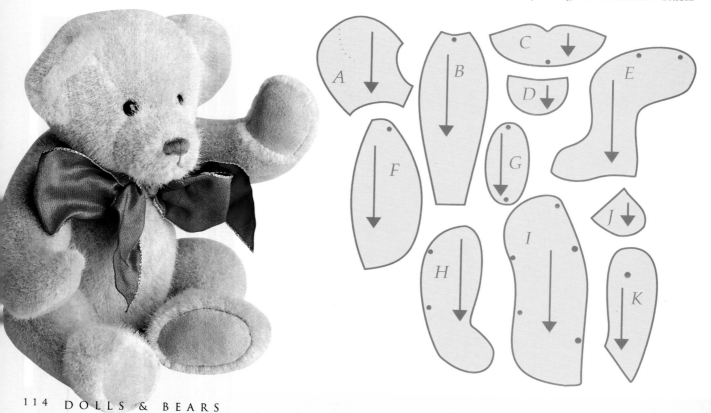

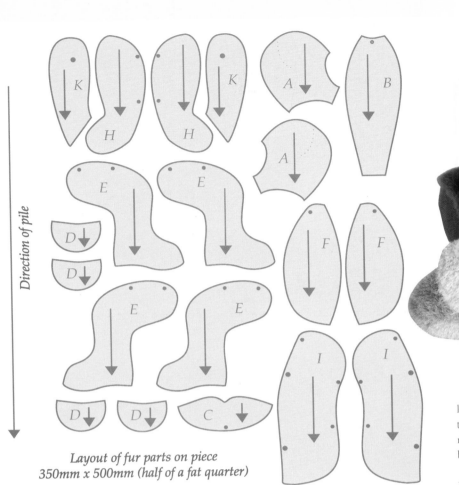

Direction of pile

**Layout of fur parts on piece
350mm x 500mm (half of a fat quarter)**

otherwise specified, all seams are stitched with right sides together.

Join Head Gusset to Side Heads, matching symbols. Matching point C on Muzzle to centre of Gusset, join seam D-C-D.

Fold Muzzle in half and stitch from G to H.

Turn head right side out and run a gathering thread around neck edge.

If using snap lock eyes, they should be inserted now, before the head is stuffed.

Stuff head firmly. Insert neck joint into head, pull up gathering thread and tie off securely. (Joints can be fixed in various ways: usually cotter pins or lock nuts. Whichever one you choose, it is essential to make sure they are closed very firmly as they will loosen up once the bear is stuffed.)

Sew Ears together in pairs around curved edge. Turn right side out.

Sew Ears to head, turning under raw edges, and position eyes at the point where Gusset seams join Muzzle. Insert

eyes as follows: Using sharp scissors, make a small hole in the fabric and stuffing. Thread a long doll needle with very strong thread and bring it up from the neck edge through the hole, thread through the eye and return needle through the same hole to neck edge. Pull eye firmly down into head to create a small depression and tie off securely.

Clip fur pile from nose triangle area. Embroider the nose and mouth using two strands of brown cotton. Outline the nose area with a triangle of straight stitches, then fill in with close satin stitch worked horizontally. Next, work a second row of vertical satin stitch over the first. Finally, outline the nose again with straight stitches and complete the mouth, as photographed.

Stitch centre front seam of Side Fronts, then stitch centre back seam of Side Backs, leaving opening as indicated. Stitch front to back at side and turn right side out through centre back opening.

Join Legs together in pairs, leaving opening in top edge, as indicated, and

leaving foot edge open. With right sides together, stitch Foot Pad to each Leg, matching leg seams to centre front and back of each Pad. Turn right side out.

Stitch Paw Pad to lower end of each Inner Arm, then stitch Inner Arm to Outer Arm, leaving an opening for turning, as indicated. Turn right side out.

Join arms and legs to body as marked, inserting joints into the limbs first, and then through to the body.

Join head to body. Stuff body and limbs firmly. Polyester filling, pellets or a mixture of both can be used for stuffing.

Use a stuffing stick, or blunt tool, to pack stuffing down firmly, working carefully to shape and mould each piece to your satisfaction.

Close openings with ladder stitch, as follows: Using strong thread, pick up a few threads of fabric along the seam-line on one side, then pick up the same distance along the other side of the opening. The crossover thread represents a rung of the ladder, and the pick-up sections represent the side supports. (See diagram page 108.)

As long as strong thread is used, several stitches can be worked and then tightened really firmly to pull the two sides together securely.

Trim the muzzle fur if desired and trim finished teddy with a neck bow.

BERTIE THE BEAR

Measurements

Height 22cm using Masquerade;
18cm using Grampian Chunky.

Materials

- 1 x 100g ball Hayfield Grampian Chunky OR 2 x 50g balls Hayfield Masquerade
- One pair of 4.50mm (No 7) knitting needles
- Polyester fibre filling
- Ribbon
- Scraps of black yarn for features

Abbreviations

See **Knitting and Crochet Notes** on page 120.

Back

Note. Bear is worked in garter stitch throughout.
Cast on 8 sts.
Inc one st at beg of next 12 rows...20 sts.**
Dec one st at each end of foll 4th rows 4 times... 12 sts.
Work 4 rows.
Cast off.

Front

Work as for back to **.
Next row. *K2, inc in next st; rep from * to last 2 sts, K2...26sts.
Dec one st at each end of 3rd and every foll alt row until 12 sts rem.
Work 4 rows.
Cast off.

Head Side Piece

Make two. Cast on 12 sts.
Knit 2 rows.
Next row. Inc in first st, knit to end.

Next row. Knit to last st, inc in last st.
Rep last 2 rows once more...16 sts.
Knit 2 rows.
Cast off 2 sts at beg of next and foll alt rows...12 sts.
Knit 2 rows.
Dec one st at each end of nect 2 rows...8 sts. Cast off.

Head gusset

Cast on 6 sts.
Inc one st at each end of foll 4th rows 3 times...12 sts.
Knit 8 rows.
Dec one st at beg of next 6 rows...6 sts.
Knit 7 rows.
Next row. *K2tog; rep from * to end...3 sts. Cast off.

Ears

Cast on 10 sts.
Knit 2 rows.
Dec one st at beg of next 4 rows...6 sts.
Knit one row.
Inc one st at beg of next 4 rows...10 sts.
Knit 2 rows.
Cast off.

Arms

Cast on 18 sts.
Knit 9 rows.
Dec one st at beg of next 2 rows...16 sts.
Knit 2 rows.
Next row. K7, K2tog, K7...15 sts.
Dec one st at each end of next 2 rows...11 sts.
Cast off.

Legs

Cast on 22 sts.
Inc one st at beg of next 4 rows...26 sts.
Dec one st at each end of next 4 rows...18 sts.
Knit 8 rows.
Next row. K8, K2tog, K8...17 sts.
Dec one st at each end of next 2 rows...13 sts.
Cast off.

To make up

Join Back and Front, leaving neck edge open; fill body. Fold Arms and Legs in half, join seams leaving cast-off edges open.
Fill limbs and stitch cast-off edges in position to body.
Stitch Head Gusset between Head Side Pieces; join under chin. Fill Head and stitch to neck edge of body, drawing up edges to form neck.
Fold ears in half and gather along cast-on and cast-off edges; sew in position.
Embroider face as illustrated.
Tie ribbon around neck.

SWEET AND SIMPLE

Here's a dear little bear, just right for a newcomer to the family, and so easy even big sister can make him!

Watch out for— *Soft*

Furnishings
AND DESIGNER TRIMS

*Redecorating made easy.
Practical and inspirational,
the revised edition of Soft Furnishings
is an essential reference for the
up-to-date home library.*

Featuring

* BED LINEN * CUSHIONS * TRIMS
* FURNITURE COVERS * TABLE LINEN * LAMPSHADES
* WINDOW DRESSING

The individual touch!

INSTRUCTIONS

SEWING NOTES

Most patterns for the sewing featured are provided on the pull-out pattern sheets accompanying the book.

Before you trace pattern pieces for the design you have chosen, check the scale diagram to make sure you are tracing the correct pieces. Each piece is marked with a number, or individually named, the same on both the scale diagram and the pattern sheet.

Numbers on the borders of the pattern sheet will help you find the corresponding piece on the sheet.

To trace patterns, use either semi-transparent sheets of paper over pattern sheet, or place pattern sheet on a sheet of plain wrapping paper and use a tracing wheel to outline each piece. (If using a tracing wheel, make sure to work on a surface that won't be damaged.)

Key

Centre fold lines are marked by broken lines. Lines or dots indicate the position of pockets and other openings (usually in a seam). These are shown on all relevant pieces.

Note. Seam allowances must be added to all patterns when cutting, unless it is otherwise specified.

KNITTING NOTES

Tension

Correct tension is essential. If your tension is not exactly as specified in the pattern, your garment will be the wrong size. Before starting any pattern, make a tension swatch, at least 10cm square. If you have more stitches to 10cm in width than is recommended, use larger needles or hook. If you have fewer stitches to 10cm than recommended, use smaller needles or hook.

Knitting abbreviations

Alt: alternate; **beg:** begin/ning; **cm:** centimetre/s; **cont:** continue; **dec:** decrease, decreasing; **foll:** following; **garter st:** knit every row; **inc:** increase, increasing; **incl:** including, inclusive; **K:** knit; **0:** no rows, stitches or times; **patt:** pattern; **P:** purl; **psso:** pass slipped stitch over; **p2sso:** pass 2 slipped sts over; **rem:** remain/s, remaining, remainder; **rep:** repeat; **rnd/s:** round/s; **sl:** slip; **st/s:** stitch/es; **st st:** stocking st (knit row on right side, purl row on wrong side); **tbl:** through back of loop; **tog:** together; **ybk:** yarn back (take yarn back under the needle from purling position); **yft:** yarn front

(bring yarn under needle from the knitting position to purling position); **yfwd:** yarn forward (bring yarn under the needle then over into knitting position again, thus making a stitch); **yrn:** yarn around needle (take yarn around needle into purling position, thus making a stitch).

Knitting graphs

Knit odd-numbered (right side) rows and purl even-numbered (wrong side) rows unless otherwise stated.

TABLE OF BRITISH EQUIVALENTS

Wool

8-ply = DK,
10-ply = Aran

12-ply = Sport or Chunky,
14-ply = Chunky

Knitting needles

UK Size	Metric Size (mm)	UK Size	Metric Size (mm)
000	10	7	4.5
00	9	8	4
0	8	9	3.75
1	7.5		3.5
2	7	10	3.25
3	6.5	11	3
4	6	12	2.75
5	5.5	13	2.25
6	5		

ACKNOWLEDGEMENTS

Photography by Andre Martin, Valerie Martin, Joe Filshie, Catherine Muscat, Andrew Elton.

Toys and clothes designed by Alison Bushell, Georgina Bitcon, Maria Ragan, Jenny Bradford, Ariadne, Libelle, Betty Smith.

Heirloom dolls, Sugar Britches and Gumdrop from Sarah Sey Dolls, 39 Annangrove Rd, Kenthurst, NSW 2156. Oscar, Lucinda and Scallywag bears from Gerry's Teddies, 30 John Street, Rosewood, Qld 4340.

Doll, page 43, courtesy of the Doll Collectors' Club of NSW.